# PANHANDLE PILOT

## Twenty Years of Flying in Southeast Alaska

## By Bob Adkins

# PANHANDLE PILOT

Library of Congress Control Number: 2012943482

ISBN: 978-1-57833-574-9

First Printing July 2012

Printed by Bang Printing in the United States through **Alaska Print Brokers**, Anchorage, Alaska.

Book & Cover design: Vered R. Mares, 𝕿𝖔𝖉𝖉 𝕮𝖔𝖒𝖒𝖚𝖓𝖎𝖈𝖆𝖙𝖎𝖔𝖓𝖘
Copy Editor: Jen Coffey
Photographs: Bob Adkins

This book was typeset in 12 pt. Adobe Jenson Pro font.

Published by
PANHANDLE PUBLISHING
P.O. Box 455
Haines, Alaska 99827
Tel: (907) 766-2294
e-mail: bobadkinsfoto@aptalaska.net
web: www.bobadkinsphotography.com

Distributed by
𝕿𝖔𝖉𝖉 𝕮𝖔𝖒𝖒𝖚𝖓𝖎𝖈𝖆𝖙𝖎𝖔𝖓𝖘
611 E. 12th Ave.
Anchorage, Alaska 99501
Tel. (907) 274-8633 • Fax (907) 929-5550
e-mail: sales@toddcom.com • WWW.ALASKABOOKSANDCALENDARS.COM

with other offices in Ketchikan, Juneau and Fairbanks, Alaska

# TABLE OF CONTENTS

North

Southeast
Alaska

Scale: 1"=105 miles

# FOREWORD

Bob Adkins is my long-time friend, partner, and an all around nice guy. We met near Wasilla, Alaska, in 1968. Bob and his wife Aleta had a little girl, Denise. My wife Lenere and I had a little boy, Wes. Bob and I hit it off immediately. Bob had recently moved to Anchorage to teach at West High School. He and Aleta had met and married in Sitka, Alaska, where they were both high school teachers. Bob learned to fly a float plane in Southeast Alaska and earned his private pilot's license in 1967.

I had gone to airplane mechanics school and had been working for Northwest Airlines in Minneapolis. In April 1968 I moved my family to Anchorage so I could fulfill my boyhood dream of hunting, fishing and flying in Alaska. Bob and I started talking about hunting, fishing and flying as soon as we met, and we've been doing it ever since.

In 1969 I bought a damaged Cessna 170A for $2200, began re-pairing it in my spare time, and by 1970 I had her ready to go. That November Bob and I took off in the 170 from Anchorage, bound for Montague Island. Though very inexperienced, we wanted to do some deer hunting.

I didn't know what to expect, but I had heard that you could land on the beach with an airplane! When we arrived I started flying the beach and soon found a set of airplane tire tracks in the beach sand. I figured that if some other airplane had landed there, I could land there too. Little did I realize that the other airplane could have been a Super Cub with large tires. In spite of our heavier airplane and smaller tires we made the landing OK, and were soon headed into the woods on my first Alaskan hunting venture.

We hunted open grassy meadows with scattered stands of large spruce and hemlock trees and had an awesome view of Prince William Sound. About noon we headed back to the airplane, having seen no deer but lots of sign.

We spread our lunch out on the tail of the airplane and began to eat. After a few minutes we looked down the beach and discovered that two deer had come out onto the beach a couple of hundred yards away. We decided Bob would take one and I would take the other. Shortly we were dressing the two deer. We packed them to the plane, threw them in, and soon were off the beach flying out over the beautiful blue waters of Prince William Sound for the 100 mile flight home. Talk about depending on your engine!

As we were flying back over the awesomely beautiful Alaskan landscape with our game in the back I could hardly believe that at the age of 23 I was in Alaska, had my own airplane, and was on a hunting trip with a great friend who could fly and help keep us out of trouble. Bob and I had quite a few more good trips in the old 190 horsepower Cessna 170A.

On long winter evenings Bob and I often sat and talked about moving to Haines, Alaska, because it was one of the most beautiful places either of us had ever seen. Haines was not your best place to get a good job or to make a lot of money. As a matter of fact there were very few jobs there, but that did not slow us down any, so with no job and no real prospects Bob, Aleta, and their two daughters moved to Haines in the fall of 1974, and my family followed in the late spring of 1975.

The summer of 1975 found Bob and me commercial fishing for red salmon in Bristol Bay out of Naknek, Alaska. One particularly windy day as we were fishing near the mouth of the Kvichak River a large wave hit our boat, the Aleta Kay, broadside and I was thrown overboard. I was wearing full rain gear, rubber boots and no life jacket! When I came up I could see that Bob hadn't seen me go over. I yelled to him and was able to swim to the side of the boat and grab a tire that was used as a bumper. With much struggle and determination Bob was able to get me back on board, saving my life! Most people who fall overboard in Bristol Bay never live to tell the story, as the tides are fast and I can personally testify that the water is cold!

After we completed the fishing season Bob and I traveled back home to start our new venture of living in Haines. Bob had gotten a job teaching school, and I planned to open an airplane maintenance shop.

Over the years Bob and I were partners in two or three airplanes. We never had any written agreements on anything. We just said, "You do this, and I will do that" and a handshake was good enough.

We also partnered on a commercial fishing operation. Bob owned a Southeast Alaska gillnet permit. After school started each year he would transfer the permit to me, so I could fish the fall chum and silver salmon season. The permit was worth about $50,000 and state law required that there be no encumbrances on a permit, but again, our word to each other was good enough. After fishing was over in the fall, I would transfer the permit back to him.

The years in Haines were wonderful years with the Adkins as our friends. We were all together at least two or three times a week. We would often have picnics on the beach with them and other friends. Bob taught our son Wes, in junior high, and coached him in the school's rifle club. He once wrote on Wes's report card "If Wes would pay as much attention to math as he does to thinking about hunting, fishing and trapping, he would get somewhere in school." I bet Bob was a fine one to talk about that, as I can guess that he was the same way when he was a kid.

Bob and I had many great times together, and I don't remember that there was ever any cross words or disagreements between us.

In 1985 Reggie Radliffe and I formed a flying company called Haines Airways, which you will read about in this book. We hired Bob as an air taxi pilot. It was wonderful to have him as a line pilot because I always had confidence that he would deliver our passengers and come home safely. Flying on-demand air service in Southeast Alaska is probably one of the toughest areas in the world to fly. I spent many worrisome hours concerned that our pilots and passengers would be safe, but I never worried too much about Bob as I knew him well and knew he had excellent decision-making skills and a lot of experience to back it up.

Reggie and I sold Haines Airways in 1987, and the company went on to grow from our three airplanes to seven or eight. Bob flew for 12 years total without an accident, incident or even a scratch on a company airplane --- what a great record of flying in Southeast Alaska.

We moved back to Anchorage in 1987, and I have been working for the FAA since 1996. Bob and Aleta are still in Haines, but they get to Anchorage at least once or twice a year and we try to get out for a Mexican dinner together and tell ... guess what ... hunting and fishing and flying stories and reminisce about the old times and all the fun we had.

Bob is a great guy, and this is a great book. You can rest assured that every word in this book is true. Any pilot, commercial fisherman and teacher that has not only survived, but done it with flying colors in Alaska for almost 45 years doesn't need to embellish the stories. The truth is better than fiction.

*Ernie Walker*
Wasilla, Alaska
July, 2008

# PREFACE

PANHANDLE PILOT is a collection of aviation-related stories - a record of some of the more memorable things that I experienced during my flying years, or in a couple of cases, stories related to me by impeccable sources that I enjoyed so much that I just had to pass them on.

While you read these anecdotes, please keep in mind several things. First, while I originally learned to fly at 26, my "career" as an air taxi pilot started when I was 45 years old, married and had two teen-age daughters. Many pilots begin flying commercially at a much younger age, so it's not unusual to have a 20-year-old air taxi pilot, and this is sometimes where the question of "judgment" enters the picture. Remember, there's a reason why auto insurance is so high for male drivers under 25 years of age.

Second, throughout my flying career, air taxi work was a summer job for me. I also had a satisfying and rewarding career in education, and while my pilot friends were fighting fog, snow, freezing rain and other such winter hazards, I was warm and dry in a classroom or administrative office, immersed in the task of trying to educate junior high school kids, a job with its own set of obstacles and hazards. *(One of my education co-workers used to state emphatically that "junior high isn't an 'age' ... it's a disease!")*

Third, 99% of these events took place in Alaska, and most of them in Southeast Alaska, one of the most beautiful and rugged areas in North America. This is a land that will get hold of a person, as it did with me, and keep them here in spite of the weather, the isolation and the inconveniences. While I don't stress it in these stories, I sincerely hope that my love of this land shows through. Robert Service had it exactly right when he wrote:

> There's the land. (Have you seen it?)
> It's the cussedest land that I know,
> From the big, dizzy mountains that screen it
> To the deep, deathlike valleys below.
> Some say God was tired when He made it;
> Some say it's a fine land to shun;
> Maybe; but there's some as would trade it
> For no land on earth — and I'm one.
> *The Spell of the Yukon* ©1940

Finally, in a number of these stories the names have been changed to protect the innocent, the not so innocent and/or the shy and retiring. A few locales were altered also, for the same reasons, but the stories, while not necessarily in chronological order, are all true.

# Chapter One
## BACKGROUND

The 300 horsepower Lycoming engine rumbled smoothly along as I leveled off at 2500 feet over Funter Bay, headed almost due west out of Juneau for Hoonah. Straight ahead the early morning sun, just rising over the Juneau Icecap behind me, illuminated the stark, magnificently craggy and snowcapped Fairweather Range. Mt. Fairweather (15,300 ft.) and Mt. Crillon (12,700 ft.) dominated the skyline to the northwest beyond Glacier Bay. In the far distance I could see the Pacific Ocean between some of the lower mountain peaks and beyond the mouth of Icy Strait.

To my left Chatham Strait ran south between Admiralty Island and Chichagof Island, both considerably bigger than the state of Rhode Island but each with permanent populations of under 1500 people. Both islands are heavily timbered along the bays, beaches and lower elevations, with rugged mountains, snowcapped much of the year, dominating their interior regions.

Over my right wing I could see 50 miles to the north up Lynn Canal, the longest, deepest and most beautiful fjord in North America. At its head, just beyond my view, were the small communities of Haines (population 2,300) and Skagway (population 800), each literally surrounded and hemmed in by the majestic mountains of Southeast Alaska's Coast Range.

I glanced again at the Cherokee's instrument panel, saw that everything was as it should be, and settled back to enjoy the scenic 20-minute flight to Hoonah.

I had left Haines for Gustavus at 5:30 a.m. that morning, with four passengers for the Glacier Bay day-boat trip that departs Bartlett Cove at 7:00 a.m. In Gustavus I picked up three people who had been kayaking in Glacier Bay. They were headed for Juneau and eventually back home to the Lower 48.

Now I had a load of freight and groceries to deliver in Hoonah, and then a deadhead back to Haines for a midmorning Glacier Bay flightseeing tour.

As I cruised along in smooth air and blue skies, I couldn't help thinking to myself "This has got to be one of the greatest jobs in the world," and reflected back on the events that made it possible for me to be where I was, since my aviation "career" had developed in a slightly less than normal manner.

For instance, my first solo flight was very nearly the last flight I ever made. I almost collided with the Fairbanks Airport control tower. Let me give you a little background first, and then I'll tell you all about it.

Like so many other boys, I've been fascinated by flight for as long as I can remember. When I was still very small I used to stop dead in my tracks, along with every other kid in my neighborhood, and watch openmouthed every time an airplane went over our house. My first flight occurred when I was seven years old. My dad paid $5 for a half-hour scenic flight for the two of us over Benton Harbor, Michigan, the nearest town to our home with an airport. The airplane was a Piper of some sort, a PA-12 I think, because even today, over sixty years later, I can picture the fabric covering of the high wings and fuselage, one pilot's seat in front and two passenger seats in back. I still recall the thrill of leaving the ground and looking down at the roads, houses and cars below.

During my upper elementary and junior high school years I made all kinds of model airplanes from kits that were composed of dozens of sticks and sheets of balsa wood, templates for stringers and spacers that had to be cut out with a razor blade and then glued together, huge pieces of tissue paper that were eventually supposed to cover the balsa framework, and bottles of airplane "dope" to tighten and harden the tissue paper.

My early attempts looked a lot like you would expect, but a few of them actually did bear a superficial resemblance to an airplane. Some of the models were rubber-band powered, and when one of them would actually take flight and fly a few feet, I would be pleased beyond words. They usually didn't last many flights, as the hazards to aviation in my rural backyard were great, and those models were very fragile.

By the time I was in junior high school I had read every aviation book in our school library, as well as exhausting the resources of Stevensville, Michigan's (*population 500*) small public library. I was well acquainted with the exploits of the Flying Tigers, Guadalcanal's Blacksheep Squadron, Midway, The Battle of Britain and many other WW II aviation sagas. I knew about Charles Lindbergh and Amelia Earhart, Anton Saint Exupéry and Eddie Rickenbacker, Italian and Russian aviation exploits, Alaska bush pilots, flight around the world, etc.

I even persuaded my dad to switch from Lucky Strikes® to Wings® brand cigarettes for a couple of years, because Wings gave aviation trading cards with every pack. I had a complete set of their trading cards. I wish I still had that set today. It would be worth a lot of money. I could identify Mustangs, Corsairs, Hellcats, P-38s, Zeros, Messerschmitts, Spitfires, Hurricanes, Focke Wulfs, B-17s, B-24s, B-25s, B-26s, B-29s and who-knows-what-else at a glance, just from studying my Wings trading cards. Shortly after that, dad had a cancer scare and quit smoking. At the time I was glad I had finished my trading card collection. Later I was just glad he quit.

In high school I took all of the math and science classes I could. I was a better-than-average student, and earned good grades all through school. I knew that my folks were not going to be able to afford to send me to college, but I reasoned that if I could get an appointment to one of the military academies, not only would I get a free college education, but I would also have the opportunity to learn to fly. All I had to do was convince one of my state congressmen to appoint me. *(Hah! That just shows how naïve I was.)* My enthusiasm grew even greater when the U.S. Air Force Academy opened in 1955, my sophomore year of high school.

Early in my senior year I applied for an appointment to the fledgling Air Force Academy, took the competitive exams, and scored well enough academically to be in the running for an appointment.

The next hurdle was the physical exam. My dad and I traveled all the way across Michigan to Selfridge Air Force Base near Detroit, and I underwent my first flight physical the following day. The results were mostly positive, but at the same time devastating. I had a correctable irregularity in my nasal system *(the result of a car accident a couple of years earlier)*, AND I was partially color-blind.

Being color-blind meant that while I could still attend the Air Force Academy, and still be a member of a flight crew, I could never become an Air Force pilot. Military pilots had to have perfect color vision. I was disappointed beyond words, and gave up the idea of attending a military academy almost immediately. I wanted to *fly*, not just ride around in someone else's airplane.

I graduated in 1958, a member of the first class to graduate from Lakeshore High School in Stevensville. Lakeshore High was the result of the 1957 merger of the Stevensville School District and the nearby Baroda School District. June of 1958 found me with no real plans for the future, and no resources beyond a high school diploma and a 1950 Oldsmobile coupe of somewhat questionable reliability.

I applied for a number of jobs around the area, but the job market was really tight, and the only thing I could come up with was a dishwashing job at Win Shuler's, a large upscale restaurant catering to the resort crowd that frequented nearby Lake Michigan beaches during the summers.

It didn't take too many weeks of dishwashing for me to see the handwriting on the wall. In September I made arrangements with the restaurant to work part-time and registered for engineering courses at nearby Benton Harbor Community College. For the next two years Shuler's manager, Jack Finlayson, very kindly allowed me to work, mainly as a busboy and part-time cook, during the evenings, weekends, and summers. I attended college classes full time during the school year.

In the fall of 1960 I transferred to the University of Michigan in Ann Arbor, and declared a major in aeronautical engineering. During that school year I realized that engineering was going to keep me working with equations and slide rules (*That's pretty dated, eh?*), while I really preferred working with people. The following year I transferred again, this time to Western Michigan University in Kalamazoo, where I again went to school during the day, and worked nights and summers at various jobs, both on-campus and off.

My major at WMU was secondary education, with emphasis in math and physics. I found that I really liked teaching and working with young people, so when I graduated in January 1963 I decided to continue on and get my master's degree in school counseling. Three semesters later (*spring 1964*) I was back in a very familiar place - graduation approaching, no job and no money, only this time I had three more diplomas and a slightly more reliable 1955 Pontiac. What was I going to do?

My serious girl friend of the past several years had recently and unexpectedly broken up with me and moved to California. I had no other strong emotional ties to consider, and I had long been fascinated with Alaska. What better place to go for awhile, to forget a disappointing relationship and to hunt, fish and experience the places and adventures that I had so often read about in outdoor magazines? I got a map of Alaska, noted every town that was on Alaska's sparse highway system, and started sending letters of inquiry for teaching positions to Alaska's school districts. My plan was to spend a couple of years in Alaska, and then return to a "real life" back in Michigan.

As it turned out, Alaska was starving for teachers. On March 28, 1964, the day after Alaska's Good Friday earthquake, I received a telegram from the Sitka Borough School District offering me a high school math position. They had never laid eyes on me and didn't ask for an interview or anything, not even a phone call. They responded to my letter of inquiry with a contract offer, which I promptly accepted, figuring that a bird in the hand was worth two in the bush. As it happened, I received seven more contract offers by mail during the following week. Sitka won (*or lost, depending on one's viewpoint*) by sending a telegram instead of using the post office.

In July of 1964 I traded my Pontiac in on a brand new Ford F-250 pickup, built a weatherproof canopy on it with my dad's help, loaded all my earthly possessions in the back, and started off for Alaska with a friend from college, Bill Willavize, who was going along just for the experience. We planned to camp the whole way.

Six weeks later Bill and I had driven the Alaska Highway (*1,300 miles of gravel, dust and mud*), visiting Whitehorse, Tok and Fairbanks along the way. We went hunting along the Denali Highway (*worse gravel, if possible*) where I killed a huge bull caribou. We stopped a few days in Anchorage, then drove down and fished for salmon in the Kenai River. Bill harvested a black bear while we were on the Kenai. We finally made the loop back through Glenallen and Tok, backtracked down the Alaska Highway to Haines Junction, and took the Haines Cutoff to Haines, where we boarded the Alaska state ferry for Sitka.

Originally I was so ignorant that I thought Sitka and the rest of the communities in Southeast Alaska were accessible by road because the map I was using indicated that they were on the Alaska Marine Highway. I didn't realize that "marine highway" meant access was by ferry only (*or by air*). I had soon realized my mistake, but as it turned out I greatly appreciated Sitka, and had already fallen in love with the rugged wilderness beauty of Alaska.

During the next two years I had opportunity to fish for halibut and salmon, hunt deer and brown bear almost in my back yard. I also made a couple of successful late summer hunting trips up into the Interior that resulted in shooting a moose and a near-recordbook 40+ inch Dall sheep.

By this time I had become Sitka High School's guidance counselor. I really liked my job and the Sitka school system. I had a wonderful new girl friend, a fellow high school teacher named Aleta Tice. I acquired a 26 foot cabin cruiser, and had all the hunting and fishing opportunities a person could ask for. I was content ... I thought.

# Chapter Two
## FIRST SOLO

University of Alaska Fairbanks (UAF) sent out invitations in the spring of 1966 for an NDEA (*National Defense Education Act*) eight-week Intensive Summer Institute for school counselors. I was very interested in furthering my education at that point, so I applied and was accepted, along with approximately 30 other school counselors from all over the U.S. The course was to run from early June to early August, which meant it would be over just in time for the opening of hunting season on August 10. What could be more perfect?

I arranged to room in the UAF dormitory with Jim Fleming, a friend of mine who had arrived in Sitka at the same time I did, and then moved to Anchorage the following year. We started classes in the Institute, and both rapidly came to two conclusions: 1) dormitory food at UAF was pretty much on a par with most other dorm cafeterias we had experienced, and 2) the Institute was indeed interesting and informative, but there was very little work to be done outside of attending classes. In other words, we had lots of free time, and spent quite a bit of it searching for different gastronomical delights available in the greater Fairbanks area.

In our quest for non-dorm meals, we discovered that the Fairbanks airport had a good restaurant. On one of our dinnertime jaunts to the airport we decided to drive up and down the flight line. This was long before the days of "airport security." Fairbanks had a goodly number of small aircraft, fascinating to me, of course, so I really enjoyed idling slowly along and "gawking" at all the airplanes.

Most of the planes were Piper "Cubs" ... PA-11s, -12s, -14s or -18s (*I couldn't tell the difference then*), or Cessnas ... 140s, 170s or 180s. I could recognize a few, but not all - the Wings® trading cards had only covered military, not civilian, aircraft. There was one, a nice shiny new-looking low wing job, parked beside a small shack that had a sign advertising "Flight Instruction - $10/ hour." Hmmmm ... that was intriguing, so I pulled over so we could take a closer look at this airplane.

Jim wasn't nearly as interested as I was, but still we walked around it once or twice, and looked through the windows at the cockpit and instrument panel. About that time a beat-up old pickup truck stopped and a smiling man got out and asked "Are you interested in learning to fly?" One comment led to another. I began asking questions, and soon I had learned that this fellow was Don Jonz, the owner of the airplane we were looking at, and a flight instructor and charter service operator. Likewise, he learned my name and told me how to get a flight physical and a student pilot's license. I made an appointment with him to have my first flying lesson on the evening of July 9, 1966.

Piper Cherokee 140, N7011 Romeo, and I got along like strawberries and cream. It was love at first sight. The Cherokee was simple to fly, responsive, and very stable. I took to flying like a duck takes to water. Being airborne was one of the most fantastic and exciting experiences I'd ever had.

By July 17, according to my brand new log book, I had experienced a familiarization flight, stalls, slow flight, low flight, turns and banks, basic instrument flight and takeoffs and landings, and had a grand total of 4.4 hours. Don was apparently pleased with my progress. That evening, after shooting a couple of touch-and-go landings, he directed me to taxi over in front of the tower and said "Take it around the pattern three times by yourself. I'll go over and watch you from the control tower," and got out of the airplane and walked away.

Man, oh man!!! "Take it around by yourself!" Don said. That means ... SOLO! Shades of the Wright brothers ... The Battle of Britain ... Off We Go, Into The Wild Blue Yonder ... Charles Lindbergh in the Spirit of St. Louis ... Flying Tigers ... I was *REALLY* excited!!!

I got myself settled down again, and then called the tower and asked for permission to taxi back to the active runway.

"Fairbanks tower, One One Romeo, taxi for takeoff with the numbers. Staying in the pattern."

"One One Romeo, taxi runway 19. You're number two behind the Alaska Airlines jet. Hold short of the active."

"One One Romeo, roger," and down the taxiway I went. I was excited and apprehensive at the same time as I ran through the takeoff checklist in my mind. The jet ahead of me pulled immediately onto the runway, opened the throttles, and started his takeoff roll, spewing great clouds of black smoke behind each engine. Halfway down the runway the jet rotated, lifted smoothly into the calm evening air, and departed for points unknown.

"One One Romeo, cleared for takeoff. Be aware of wake turbulence from the departing jet."

"One One Romeo, roger."

Wake turbulence? What the heck is wake turbulence? I didn't remember ever hearing anybody mention "wake turbulence," but I was cleared for takeoff, and I was going to go flying ... solo ... all by myself! I slowly opened the throttle and started down the runway, gathering speed, working the rudder pedals to stay right on the runway center line, and gently easing back on the control wheel, just as I'd been taught.

One One Romeo broke ground, rose gracefully into the calm evening air a few feet ... and suddenly became a snarling, uncontrollable monster, as if a giant hand grabbed her and flung her away. She rolled up on her right wing and simultaneously entered a steep, shuddering right bank. I thought for sure she was going clear over on her back. Almost instantly I was WAY off the centerline of the runway, and frantically realized that Romeo and I were headed, full throttle and with the wings nearly vertical, straight for the control tower.

As I fought the controls and careened past the tower, missing it by what seemed like inches, I had the fleeting impression of several startled and wide-eyed faces looking out the windows at me. I know Don said he would watch my first solo from the tower, but I don't think this was the view he had in mind.

I had instinctively jammed full left rudder and left aileron, and could feel Romeo trying to respond as she skidded and shuddered wildly through the evening sky. After several breathless seconds, which seemed absolutely endless to me, the airplane finally and somewhat reluctantly rolled back to the left until the wings were level and straightened out of its skid, leaving me scared witless and wondering how in the world I managed to miss the control tower and get out over the airport parking lot instead of over the runway, which by then was a long way off to my left.

"One One Romeo, Fairbanks Tower. Are you OK?"

Still wide-eyed and breathless, I managed to respond (*quite coolly, I hoped*) "Fairbanks Tower, One One Romeo. Roger, I'm OK. Request permission to re-enter the pattern for touch-and-gos."

"One One Romeo, roger."

By the time I managed to maneuver Romeo back to the vicinity of the runway and climb to pattern altitude (*800 ft. AGL, above ground level*) I had resumed breathing, but I was still really wary of the aircraft going berserk again, as I had no clue what had happened. I had the control wheel in a death grip, and was convinced I was holding the airplane in the air by sheer will power alone. Romeo behaved perfectly though, and I successfully went around the traffic pattern and managed to get the airplane back on the ground without breaking anything, although my landing was anything but smooth. I took off again, and this time, since there had been no further thrills and chills, I was able to relax a little. My second go-around was much more regular and according to the book, with proper radio communication in all the right spots. My second landing was much improved, and after taking off again and going around the pattern once more I actually greased the third landing, touching down so lightly I hardly felt the wheels contact the runway. Good enough, I thought, and called the tower for a full stop, as Don had specified three touch-and-gos. I taxied Romeo to her tiedown and shut down the engine. When I got out, I was still feeling pretty shaky and my knees felt like they were going to give way and collapse.

Don arrived just as I exited the airplane, and I could tell he was tense and agitated, too.

"Why in the world did you take off right behind that jet, when the tower warned you about wake turbulence?" he asked excitedly.

"What in the world *is* wake turbulence?" I responded. "That's the second time this evening somebody has mentioned 'wake turbulence'. I've never heard of it before."

He looked a little chagrined, and said "We'll talk about it next lesson. By the way, you did a great job of recovering."

Don endorsed my logbook for 30 minutes PIC (*pilot-in-command*) time, and he wrote "First Solo" in extremely shaky letters, followed by two exclamation points. Brother, did I agree with that!

Our next lesson included a long discussion about wake turbulence and wingtip vortices. Don explained how they're generated, how to avoid them, and how dangerous they can be to small aircraft. I already had some extremely personal experience with the latter topic, which really served to drive the lesson home.

I continued flying two or three times a week. By the end of July I had logged cross-countries to Minto, Goldking, Healy, McKinley Park, Manley Hot Springs, Tanana, Circle City, Circle Hot Springs and Beaver, and had a total of 28 hours of flight time, with 17 solo. The aviation bug had bitten me hard (*almost too hard on that first solo*). When university classes ended I headed my faithful pickup south on the first leg of an early season hunting trip along the Denali Highway. Three weeks later I arrived back in Sitka, just in time for the start of the 1966-67 school year.

*Wake turbulence accidents were not uncommon in the '60s, especially when large aircraft and small aircraft shared the same runways. Not long after my first solo the FAA started requiring a minimum of three minutes between the liftoff of a large aircraft and the takeoff of smaller planes. This waiting period allows the larger plane's wake turbulence to dissipate. Flight instructors are also now required to discuss wake turbulence before a student pilot can solo.*

On October 16, 1972 Don Jonz filed a VFR flight plan from Anchorage, Alaska, to Juneau, Alaska, with four souls aboard. Flight time was listed as 3 hours and 35 minutes. He was advised that the weather on his route was below VFR minimums, but he elected to continue the flight. The aircraft disappeared, and a 39-day search, the longest in U.S. history, failed to find a trace of the airplane. Alaska's Congressional Delegate, Representative Nick Begich, and Representative Hale Boggs, the Democratic Majority Leader from Louisiana, plus Begich's personal aide, Russell Brown, were aboard the plane.

The NTSB Accident Report (1) states:

DEPARTURE POINT: ANCHORAGE, ALASKA

INTENDED DESTINATION: JUNEAU, ALASKA

TYPE OF ACCIDENT: MISSING AIRCRAFT, NOT RECOVERED

PHASE OF OPERATION: UNKNOWN/NOT REPORTED

PROBABLE CAUSE(S): MISCELLANEOUS - UNDETERMINED

REMARKS: WEATHER CONDITIONS ALONG PRESUMED ROUTE OF FLIGHT NOT CONDUCIVE TO VFR FLIGHT. PILOT COMPENSATION NOT DETERMINED. DAMAGE AND INJURIES PRESUMED.

The author and 11 Romeo, the docile Cherokee 140 that turned into an uncontrollable beast during his first solo. Flight instructor Don Jonz, Alaska Representative Nick Begich, and Louisiana Representative Hale Boggs disappeared in 1972 in the twin behind 11 Romeo.
Fairbanks, Alaska - June, 1966

## Chapter Three
## FROM WHEEL PLANE/ TO FLOAT PLANE/

After another successful caribou hunt on the Denali Highway and an exciting but unsuccessful black bear hunt on the Kenai Peninsula, I arrived back in Sitka in time for the start of the '66-'67 school year. Once again there was plenty of fishing and deer hunting to be done, plus my girl friend, Aleta, and I decided to get married, so there were lots of things going on.

I enjoyed the celebrity status of being able to say "Why yes, I'm a pilot" to my friends and acquaintances in Sitka, but by the time spring came around I was ready to go another step and seriously work towards getting my private pilot's license.

Airline passengers still arrived in Sitka, as in most other Southeast Alaska communities, via Alaska Coastal-Ellis Airlines in either a Grumman Goose or a Convair PBY. Both types were converted surplus U.S. Navy amphibious patrol/utility aircraft. They could take off and land on either a surfaced runway or water.

A PBY waits at the Sitka turnaround while a Grumman Goose taxis in. Summer, 1966

Passengers for Sitka boarded the aircraft in Juneau and took off from Juneau International Airport's paved runway. After a 30-minute flight they landed on the water in the channel between Japonski Island and the town of Sitka. Since the pilots didn't always remember to tell their passengers that they would be landing on water in Sitka, arrivals were often punctuated by shrieks and screams from panicky first-timers who thought the plane had crashed and was sinking.

An Alaska Coastal Airlines PBY landing in the channel between Sitka and Japonski Island. Mt. Edgecumbe is in the background. Summer, 1966

All private or charter aircraft in Sitka were also, by necessity, capable of taking off and landing on water. These airplanes were always high wing, had a pair of large cumbersome looking floats installed in place of wheels, and were referred to as "floatplanes," not seaplanes . The two air taxi companies in town each had their own maintenance and docking facilities, while the city furnished and maintained a public floatplane dock located between Thompson Harbor and ANB Harbor.

One of the floatplanes on the public dock, a fabric-covered tandem-seat *(front and back)* 115 h.p. Champion Citabria, N8367 Victor, was owned by the Sitka Flying Club. A few judicious questions led me to the club's current president, a local storeowner, who told me that a membership in the club cost $300 and was transferable. In other words, a share in the ownership of 67 Victor could be bought or sold by a club member.

Members signed up for desired flight times on a first come-first serve basis, and paid the club $20 a month dues, which included one free hour of flight time. Additional flights cost $8 per hour wet *(including gasoline and oil)*, and members had to agree to help during the aircraft's mandatory annual inspections. I walked out of the store $300 poorer, but owner of a share of 67 Victor, a floatplane that I couldn't yet fly, because floatplanes require entirely different takeoff and landing techniques than wheel planes.

I quickly scheduled some sessions in 67 Victor with one of the local flight instructors, so my first Sitka log book entry, dated March

2, 1967, reads "Preflights, Takeoffs and Landings, Glassy Water," and the next entry, six days later, reads "Glassy Water Approaches, Step Taxi, Water Handling, Short Field Takeoffs, Full Stall Landings, and Turns." Subsequent entries on the next two days include "Crosswind Landings, Spot Landings, Emergency Go Arounds" and finally, after almost five hours of instruction, "Supervised Solo." It was signed by Ken Bussell, CFI, and allowed me to fly 67 Victor solo, but I still couldn't take passengers unless they happened to be certified pilots or flight instructors.

During the next four months I explored the surrounding countryside by air, visiting Goddard Hot Springs, Silver Bay, Shelikof Bay, Redoubt Bay, Juneau, and a host of other places, some urban and some remote. I searched for deer and brown bear on the beaches, looked for whales in Sitka Sound, landed and fished for steelhead in some of the bigger freshwater streams and continually honed my flying skills.

The author and 67 Victor, Sitka Flying Club's Citabria on floats. Plotnikof Lake - August, 1967

I also purchased a copy of Jeppesen's excellent programmed Private Pilot Written Examination Study Guide, and after a few weeks of study passed the Private Pilot Written Exam with a score of 92%. Several hours of further flight instruction with Ken prepared me for the Private Pilot Flight Test. On July 25, 1967 E.H. Miller, the FAA flight examiner from Juneau, endorsed my log book "Private Pilot

Test OK." I was a full-fledged licensed private pilot, SES (*Single Engine, Sea*) with all the rights, privileges, and responsibilities thereof. However, my new certificate had the notation "Not valid for night flight or by color signal control," because of my color blindness. A month later I took a practical light signal test, designed to see if I could actually distinguish between the red, green, and white lights that a tower might flash at me if my radio ever went out. I passed that test with (*ahem ... if you'll pardon the pun*) flying colors, and was given a written waiver, so my license was re-issued with no limitations at all. I've used that same waiver for every other rating and flight physical that I've taken since then. It's getting pretty ragged, but it still works.

My first passenger was my bride of a few months, Aleta. We explored remote beaches and new places, made shopping trips to Juneau, visited her aunt and uncle who were logging in Gustavus to the north of us, and visited her mother and dad who cooked in a logging camp on Tuxekan Island to the south of us.

We had some very enjoyable flights. I remember how amazed we both were the first time we flew through a rainbow and discovered that, in an airplane, a rainbow forms a complete 360 degree circle.

One fine day we flew across Baranof Island and landed at Baranof Warm Springs. We enjoyed a dip in the public baths and met Wayne Short, well known Southeast homesteader and author of *The Cheechakos* and *This Raw Land*. We had read and greatly enjoyed both books, so visiting with Wayne was a real treat. Later on Wayne's son Luke was in one of Aleta's English classes at Sitka High School.

On another trip, on a sunny spring day, we were flying along a steep mountainside, and the sound of the engine set off an avalanche. A quarter-mile section of the mountain broke off and slid right out from under us, filling the valley below with great clouds of snow, and rocking us with the air currents the avalanche generated.

I learned to warn my bride about sudden attitude changes. On the way home from visiting Myron and Merie Dean, her aunt and uncle who were logging in Gustavus, we were flying over a broken layer of clouds that gradually grew denser and denser. When the layer ahead of us started looking pretty solid I decided we should go down beneath the layer.

I throttled back and started to circle down through a gap in the clouds, and immediately was grabbed from behind by my very startled wife who demanded to know "What's wrong? What's wrong? Why are we going down?"

From that time on I've tried to make it a point to inform my passengers of impending sudden maneuvers.

In addition to exploring the Alaskan countryside with my wife, I was always willing to fly anyone anywhere, as long as they paid the expenses. As a private pilot, I couldn't charge anything for my services, but it was legal for passengers to "share expenses." I flew Gail Denny, a fellow teacher, back and forth to Pelican a number of times. She had property in Pelican, and eventually retired from the classroom and opened a lodge there.

Gene Bucholtz, another fellow teacher, needed to get to Gustavus to start his summer job as a park ranger in Glacier Bay National Park. Larry Baker and his wife wanted to go to Redoubt Bay for a week long camping trip. Tom Johnson wanted some aerial photos of clear-cut logging areas for the Sitka Conservation Society. Later he and I shared several fly-in fishing trips. The list went on and on, and as the list grew longer, my aeronautical experience and total hours grew also.

Tom Johnson with a steelhead trout taken during a fly-in fishing trip. Sitkoh River - May, 1967

In late 1967, Sitka's new airport was completed, and one of the local flight instructors bought a Cessna 150, a little two-seat 100 h.p. tricycle-geared training airplane. I had the instructor check me out in the 150, and soloed it, but it was such a poor performing airplane that I only flew it a few times.

Aerial View of Sitka. The arrow indicates the location of the Sitka Municipal Floatplane Dock. Floatplanes arrived and departed in the sheltered channel between the city of Sitka and Japonski Island. The newly-completed airport is in the foreground. Sitka, Alaska – spring 1968

# Chapter Four
## ALMOST INTO THE SEA

A pilot's first hundred hours teaches him or her a lot about flying, but sometimes one doesn't even have to be airborne to learn a great lesson. I learned a lot just by watching this one.

First let me explain what a floatplane dock looks like. It's built like a regular boat dock, with a flat top surface for walking, but along one or both sides (*in Sitka's case, both sides*) there is a ramp along the whole length of the dock that slants from the upper edge of the dock down into the water at about a twenty degree angle. A float plane can slowly taxi up, perpendicular to the dock, until the front of the floats touch the slanting ramp. Then a slight goose on the throttle will power the aircraft up onto the ramp. The floats will then be completely out of the water, and the aircraft can be tied down to cleats on the dock. Needless to say, this maneuver requires the right "touch," which comes with experience. Too little throttle and you don't get up the ramp. Too much throttle, and ... oops ... over the top and down the other side you go.

Sitka's Municipal Floatplane Dock. The flying club's Citabria barreled between two tied-down aircraft, up and over the dock, and down the other side. Sitka, Alaska – summer 1994

I was standing on the floatplane dock one afternoon, waiting for 67 Victor to return from a flight. A teenage boy, a high school senior, was getting flight instruction from a local CFI (*not mine, incidentally*) who had thousands of hours and a string of certificates as long as your arm. They were shooting touch-and-gos in the channel, and had already gone well past their allotted time before finishing the lesson. The CFI instructed the teenager to make the next landing a "full stop, and taxi to the dock." The boy did as instructed, but landed quite a distance from the dock, so the instructor said to him (*as the teenager related the story later*) "There's no need to land half a mile from the dock. I'll show you how to land and taxi efficiently."

Around again they went, this time with the instructor at the controls, and came in diagonally across the channel instead of down the center. The aircraft was pointing right at the floatplane dock, and it was obvious that the instructor intended to land as close to the ramp as possible. However, the airplane floated and floated and floated, still airborne, and finally touched down about fifty yards from the float. When it hit the ramp it was still going quite fast, and zipped right up the ramp between two parked aircraft, over the top of the dock, and started down the ramp on the other side. It came to rest pointing down into the water at a twenty-degree angle, the front of the floats in the water, and the prop ticking over just a few inches above the surface. The student, sitting in the front seat, had eyes the size of saucers, but the CFI calmly shut the engine down, jumped out, and nonchalantly said "OK, let's get this thing turned around and tied down."

They had used up much of my scheduled time, and I decided that I'd already had enough entertainment for the day, so I helped them tie down the airplane, and chuckled all the way home. Since no harm or damage was done (*although the boy decided to give up flying and take guitar lessons instead*) it was an amusing incident. It could have been really serious, though, and so was a good lesson for me. It's really easy to become overconfident in your own abilities, and overconfidence causes accidents.

## Chapter Five
## BEARLY (sic) INTO THE AIR

My dad, Les Adkins, came up from Michigan to go brown bear hunting with me in early June of 1968. It was the first time I'd seen dad since I moved to Alaska four years earlier. My friend Jim Fleming flew down from Anchorage to join us. Neither of them had hunted brown bears before.

I arranged for Warren Pellett, a retired U.S. Navy pilot who lived in Sitka, to fly the three of us out to the head of Hoonah Sound, sixty-odd miles north. We planned to camp there for a week, and hunt on foot around the big grass flats in the area.

Warren had a nearly new Helio Courier on floats, one of the nicest aircraft I've ever seen. It had flaps and slats and slots and cuffs and all kinds of STOL *(short takeoff and landing)* equipment on it. The Helio is a six-place aircraft, cruises at 135 mph on floats and can maintain flight at under 35 mph. It's a fantastic airplane.

Dad (left) and Warren Pellett loading Warren's Helio for our bear hunting trip.
Sitka, Alaska – June, 1968

Warren loaded the three of us, all of our rifles, camping gear, tents, rain gear, hip boots, groceries for a week, 100 pounds of salt for bear hides, and other essential gear, into the Helio and took off for Hoonah Sound. An hour later we had all of our baggage stacked on the beach at the upper end of the south arm of the sound. We pushed the Helio back into deep water so Warren could turn around to take off, and waved goodbye. We arranged that he would pick us up seven days later.

Moser Island adjoins Chichagof Island, and at half-tide or lower a sandspit connects the north end of Moser with Chichagof. Moser Island is very narrow, and five or six miles long, dividing Hoonah Sound into a North Arm and a South Arm. We had decided to set up camp on Chichagof, right where the sandspit joins the two islands.

As we set up camp, I looked down the beach towards Moser and, lo and behold, 400 yards or so down the beach walked a huge brown bear, coming right towards us, with the breeze at his back. The only way he could get off Moser Island was to come right through our camp. As we watched the bear angled up into the narrow woods and out of our sight.

I quickly stationed dad on one side of the spit, Jim on the other, and told them I would quietly walk down the beach at the water's edge until I was sure I was past the bear and then let my scent move the bear up to the spit, where one of them was sure to get a shot at him. It worked like a charm. An hour later we were skinning dad's bear, a really handsome, very dark male that squared over nine feet.

Dad and his 9'4" brown bear. Hoonah Sound, Chichagof Island – June, 1968

The next morning we hiked down the beach and around a long, thin stand of Sitka spruce. We wanted to hunt a big grass flat with the wind in our faces. As we rounded the northern point of the trees we saw two bears traveling down the beach towards us. One was a beautiful long-haired blonde bear, the other just slightly smaller and a medium chocolate brown. We assumed (*rightly so, it turned out*) they were a boar and a sow, meandering along and grazing on the spring grasses. We sat down behind some drift logs, waited until the bears got to us, and three shots later Jim had his eight-and-a-half footer on the ground and ready to be skinned.

The smaller bear ran up into the woods, and we figured she had taken off. However, as we stood there admiring Jim's bear, she charged back out of the woods directly towards us, barely twenty yards away. We heard her running just before she broke into the open, so I had my rifle up and ready and as soon as I saw her I fired. My .375 magnum took her right under the chin, broke her spine, and killed instantly. Our bear hunt was over. Packing the heavy hides almost two miles back to camp was a chore, but with three of us taking turns it wasn't too bad.

The author and two other bears taken on the same hunt.
The bear in the rear charged the author's party. Chichagof Island – June 1968

Now we had a problem. We still had five days until Warren was supposed to pick us up, and we had three fresh bear hides to preserve. True, we had lots of salt, but the weather had turned sunny and warm, which is good for hunting bears, but not so good for preserving bear hides. Shortly after noon a fairly large boat, which I recognized as belonging to the U.S. Forest Service, came up Hoonah Sound and anchored a mile or so away from our camp. I walked over to the beach closest to them, hailed the boat, and asked them if they could radio their office in Sitka to call Warren and have him come and get us earlier, that same day, if possible.

A couple of hours later a floatplane circled over our campsite, landed and taxied up to the beach. It was Warren, all right, but he was in 67 Victor, the little two-seat club plane, not his Helio Courier. He beached the plane, jumped out, and explained that he had put the Helio in the shop for its annual inspection, and it wouldn't be flyable for another two days. He'd brought 67 Victor with the idea that he could ferry me and a load of gear back to town, and then I could ferry Dad and Jim back in separate trips. We quickly loaded a bear hide and some of our gear, and Warren flew me straight back to Sitka. I came back and got Dad, some more gear and another bear hide, and then hustled back the third time to get Jim and the rest of our stuff. It would have worked perfectly, except ...

By the time I got back to pick up Jim the wind had died down completely and the ocean was just as calm and flat as a table top. We'd also apparently left more gear for the third trip than I'd bargained for, plus I had filled 67 Victor with gas for this last round trip. By the time we got the remainder of our gear loaded and taxied out to take off, I could tell we were really, really heavy. In fact, we were so heavy that it took ages to even get up on the step. At low speed airplane floats plow through the water like displacement boat hulls. As speed increases they raise up higher and higher until they are "on the step," planing or just skimming the surface of the water. The heavier the airplane, the harder it is to get up on the step. On top of that, smooth glassy water has much more surface tension than choppy water, so it's even harder to gain speed, get on the step, and finally break loose from the surface and become airborne.

I finally managed to get one float up and out of the water. We went along like that for another mile or so, and at last 67 Victor broke water and flew. Our takeoff run must have been close to 10 miles. We were halfway down Hoonah Sound, well past the south end of Moser Island, before we were actually flying, and then we couldn't gain more than a few feet of altitude per minute.

It was a beautiful evening, with not a cloud in the sky or a ripple on the water, so we flew the whole distance back to Sitka at under a hundred feet, following the beaches all the way because we couldn't climb high enough to get over the hills between us and town. We were still so heavy that I landed in the channel at cruise power to make sure I didn't stall out during landing. Another lesson learned.

# Chapter Six
## "SEVERE WEATHER PILOTAGE"

Denise, our first daughter, was born in the winter of '67, so the following July we decided to kill two birds with one stone. Bus and Lu Tice, my in-laws, were cooking and running the mess hall at Clarence Kramer's logging camp on Tuxekan Island, 135 miles south of Sitka, on the northwest corner of Prince of Wales Island. They hadn't seen Denise yet, so I asked Warren Pellett if we could hire him to fly us down there, and then come back in a few days and pick us up again. I had already had a couple of instructional flights with Warren in his Helio. I thought that perhaps we might combine this flight with further instruction, and perhaps even get to the point where I could solo the Helio (*I'm sure this was purely wishful thinking on my part. If I had owned that Helio, I would NEVER have considered turning a 100 hour pilot loose with it*). In any case Warren agreed to fly us down, and let me fly left seat. The flight down was uneventful, in good weather, and Aleta and the baby both did fine. Warren agreed to return for us in five days.

At Friday night supper in the logging camp mess hall one of the loggers approached me and asked if I wanted to go flying the next day. I was always willing to do that, and said "Sure!" However, the situation wasn't exactly as I first pictured. This logger, Norm Aubochon, was really eager to fly. He was so eager that he had gone out and bought an airplane, a four-place Aeronca Sedan on floats, and had it delivered to the logging camp, along with several 55 gallon drums of 80/87 aviation fuel. However, he had never had a flying lesson in his life, and there was no one in camp who could or would teach him.

He wanted *me* to take *him* flying, in *his* airplane! Since I had never even seen an Aeronca Sedan before, I wasn't too sure about this. However, he had all the documentation for the airplane, and as I studied the pilot's manual, I realized that the specifications and performance parameters of the Sedan were almost identical to those of "my" airplane, 67 Victor, which made perfect sense, since Champion Aircraft Company had been resuscitated from the defunct Aeronca Aircraft Corporation a few years earlier. I figured with just two of us aboard it would handle pretty much like 67 Victor, and I was right. If anything the Sedan was more stable than 67 Victor. In fact, I liked the Sedan so well that a few years later I actually considered buying one myself.

Norm and I spent the next two beautiful days cruising around Prince of Wales Island and all the smaller nearby islands, visiting other logging camps, cruising beaches and generally having a great time. When we finished my logbook read "Tuxekan Area - Aeronca Sedan N1118H - 5.8 hr. PIC."

Sunday night our holiday with the weather ended, as a vicious Southwest storm blew in from the Pacific. There were sheets of rain, winds howling 40 and 50 mph, fog, and low ceiling and visibility. I was sure Warren would never show up in that kind of weather, but just after lunch on Monday the Helio circled the camp once, landed in the lee of a small point, and taxied to the camp dock.

Aleta and I were all for waiting for the storm to die down, but Warren had just come from Sitka and said "Oh, it's not near as bad as it looks. Come on and let's go home." He was the expert, so we hurriedly packed, loaded Denise and our luggage into the airplane, and took off for Sitka, an hour's flight away. I was again in the left seat, receiving "flight instruction."

It was instructive, all right. We soon ran into dense fog and had to turn back and try another direction. We ran into turbulence so severe that Aleta was hitting her head on the top of the cabin. We ran into gusty winds so bad that the automatic slats on the Helio's wings unexpectedly slammed open, scaring us out of a year's growth. I have a strong stomach, but I was just on the verge of being airsick the first time those slats came crashing down, and it startled me so badly that I wasn't a bit queasy for the rest of the trip.

We had to divert from our more-or-less straight-line course to Sitka due to the weather. In fact, we diverted so far that we flew right over Wrangell and Petersburg, and later on we could see the lights of Juneau. We flew all the way around the north end of Admiralty Island, and then back down to Peril Strait to come in to Sitka from the north. If you look at the map you'll see we covered over 300 miles, and the "one hour flight" went into my log book as "Tuxekan - Sitka, X-country - Severre (sic) Wx Pilotage , 2.6 hr.. , signed Warren Pellet CFI." Another lesson from the School of Hard Knocks.

## Chapter Seven
## THE LURE OF THE BIG TOWN

In August of 1968 the lure of the big city and Interior Alaska drew us, so Aleta, Denise and I moved to Anchorage, where I taught math at West High School. George Crowe, author of *Plan-A-Flight to Alaska*, was also teaching in the math department there, and often kept a number of us entertained with his flying stories during our lunch periods. He later wrote a monthly column for *Aero* magazine, and now manages FliteQuest Aviation, a large flight training school in Nampa, Idaho.

Two years later I moved to the counseling department of newly opened Service-Hanshew Secondary School, and worked there for four years. I remember clearly a lunchtime conversation that took place among several faculty members one day. Herb Niemoth, one of our school counselors in his late forties, owned a Cessna 180 on floats, and he mentioned something about having flown out to a cabin on a lake some distance west of Anchorage the previous weekend. One of the younger fellows present piped up and said "Well Herb, if you ever need anybody to go flying with you, just let me know." To which Herb succinctly replied, "Why in the world would I need anyone to go with me? My license says I'm qualified to fly all by myself."

That comment provided a lesson for several members of the group!

During our time in Anchorage I had no airplane, nor could I afford to rent a plane. Saturday afternoons often found Aleta and me driving around Lake Hood, Anchorage's huge floatplane base, but airplanes were just not in our financial picture at that point. Window shopping was all we could manage, due to other investments and the fact that teachers aren't very high on the wage scale.

We had purchased a brand new triplex apartment building on Dorbrandt Street, near Anchorage International Airport, and also welcomed our second child, Valerie, to the family. In addition, we invested in a commercial fishing boat, a 32-foot gillnetter, so I fished in Bristol Bay from early June to late July every summer.

The author's Bristol Bay gillnetter, tied up at the Whitney-Fidalgo cannery dock in the Naknek River. This is one of the main reasons the author's flying ambitions were put on hold for a few years. Naknek, Alaska – June, 1971

The only airplane stories I'll share from our time in Anchorage both involve hunting trips.

Soon after we moved to Anchorage we met Ernie and Lenere Walker. We were about the same age, and they had a little boy, Wesley, who was a year older than our daughter Denise. Ernie was an aircraft mechanic working for Anchorage Helicopters when we first met. Later he went to work for Northwestern Air Services, the Anchorage Piper dealer, so he wouldn't have to travel back and forth to the North Slope so much and could spend more time at home with his family.

We became good friends (*and still are, more than 40 years later*) and Ernie invited me on a number of hunting trips using his newly acquired Cessna 170.

Early one sunny fall morning Ernie and I left Anchorage and flew southeast out to Montague Island in the Gulf of Alaska. Montague was one of the islands that rose several feet during the Good Friday Earthquake of 1964, and as a result had many long smooth gravel beaches that were ideal landing strips for a small plane. Montague also had a sizable population of both brown bears and Sitka black-tailed deer. We were after deer.

Ernie landed on one of the long smooth beaches, and we hunted hard all morning long, up and down the hills and draws. We saw quite a bit of fresh deer sign, but we also saw many, many bear tracks. We were a little depressed as we hiked back to where the airplane was parked on the beach. We decided we would eat our lunch, and then fly to another beach to try our luck. We spread our sandwiches and cold drinks out on the tail of the airplane and had just started to eat when Ernie looked past me down the beach and quietly said "Hey, there's a deer! No, there's *two* deer!"

I slowly turned my head, and sure enough, two deer had just come out of the timber a couple of hundred yards away and were ambling down the beach toward us. "Well, shoot one of them," I said.

Ernie was already in motion, grabbing his rifle and resting it across the fuselage, just in front of the tail of the airplane. He steadied for a second, squeezed the trigger, and his deer dropped like a rock, shot through the neck.

The other deer jumped and ran a few feet and then stopped and looked back at his companion. Meanwhile I had retrieved my rifle and taken a rest across the left stabilizer. The second deer started to move towards the woods again, so I led him a little, squeezed the trigger, and at my shot it went down, shot through the lungs.

We cleaned them where they fell, taxied the airplane over to them, tossed them in the back seat, and were back in Anchorage by mid-afternoon. Both deer were young button bucks, perfect eating. It was the easiest deer hunt I've ever made, that's for sure.

Another memorable airplane hunt from our Anchorage days took place one November. The Beluga Lake area across Cook Inlet from Anchorage was open for cow moose during late season. If I remember correctly, the split season was for bulls only in September, was closed in October, and then open for cows *or* bulls in November.

In those days you could hunt the same day you were airborne. Ernie's 170 was on skis, so when we spotted a big cow with a yearling calf, we found a good sized frozen pond half a mile from them and landed. The hunt itself was simple, almost too simple. We hiked through the six-inch-deep snow and chest-high brush until we could see the two moose, and I shot the cow. We cleaned and quartered her (*actually I think we "sixthed" her*), and packed her back to the airplane.

Packing moose to the airplane at −20°F. Beluga Lake, Alaska – November, 1972

The only excitement came on the way home when we realized that a snow storm had moved into the Anchorage area, and all VFR air traffic was stopped. We had to turn around and divert a hundred miles north to Talkeetna and spend the night at the Talkeetna Roadhouse.

Next morning the weather had cleared, so we flew back to Anchorage, and there learned that a Korean Airlines cargo jet with a hundred or so live beef cattle had slid off the runway at Anchorage International Airport, crashed and burned. This happened less than a mile from my home, and for several days we could smell cooked beef whenever we went outside.

While I'm still in the hunting mode, let me tell you about the super-duper, open cockpit, low altitude, cross-country, air-cooled hunting machine I built while still living in Anchorage.

It started life as a Volkswagen Beetle, back in the '50s. I don't remember exactly what year. It was a 36 horsepower model, anyway. The rest doesn't matter, because I took the body off and the seats out and threw them away. I only kept the body pan, engine, running gear and steering wheel. The rear transaxle was replaced with one from a junked VW delivery van. The delivery vans had a lower rear end gear ratio than the passenger cars, as they were designed to haul heavier loads. The van rear end also raised the body pan an extra 4 or 5 inches, giving it more ground clearance.

With the expert help of a couple of friends, Don Carlson and Howard Hansen, I overhauled the engine, and modified the exhaust system. I welded a light steel tubing framework onto the body pan so I could attach lightweight plywood fenders, hood, and rear splash guards, and built a couple of plywood storage boxes that doubled as seats.

Oversize front tires, along with Don's ingeniously designed dual tires and wheels on the back completed the rig, and we were ready to go hunting. The buggy could take two people, camping gear, food and fuel for a week, and carry out three or four dressed caribou or a full moose easily. A rough trail or cross-country travel was no problem, and we would often follow dry gravel creek beds. Deep water (30 inches or more) or dense forest was about the only thing the buggy couldn't handle. It was perfect for the brushy tundra country that we normally hunted.

"Mudder-in-Law", my super-duper, open cockpit, low altitude, high torque, air cooled cross-country hunting machine. Built from a VW Bug, it's just rolled out of the shop, and will never look this clean again. Anchorage, Alaska – July, 1969

"Mudder-in-Law", living up to her name on a caribou hunt. Near Eureka, Alaska – August, 1971

Several of my friends, including Ernie, had similar rigs, and we spent many enjoyable days during the early August hunting seasons harvesting our meat for the winter. It often carried us fifty miles or more back into the bush, and quite frequently proved that it was appropriately named. The buggy was christened, tongue in cheek, after Aleta's mother - "Mudder-In-Law."

## Chapter Eight
## BACK IN THE BANANA BELT

Southeast Alaska is often referred to as "the Panhandle" because of its shape, or "the banana belt" because its climate is so much warmer than the rest of Alaska. As in, "It's warm enough to grow bananas" ... NOT! It's often cloudy, rainy and overcast. The sun shows itself on an average of every third or fourth day, but it may stay hidden for two or three weeks at a time. In the northern part, around Haines and Skagway, there is lots and lots of snow. As I write this there is four feet of snow on the ground. Total snowfall during any given winter will average twenty feet or more. It's not hospitable country, but it *is* some of the most wild and beautiful country in the world.

The next entry in my log book is dated July 3, 1980, showing a gap of twelve years. I didn't fly as PIC at all during our six years in Anchorage, and didn't fly for another several years after we moved to Haines.

Anchorage was growing by leaps and bounds. The trans-Alaska pipeline was about to be built, and we missed Southeast, so in July of 1974 I resigned my job at Service High School, sold our triplex, rented a Hertz truck for our furniture and belongings, packed Aleta and both girls into our crewcab pickup, and we moved to Haines. We bought an unfinished rustic A-frame cabin on the edge of town, one of only two places for sale in the whole community at the time, and the only one we could afford, and set about establishing roots in Haines.

Aerial view of Haines and the Chilkat River Valley. The Haines Airport is in the center of the photograph, just behind the town. Haines, Alaska – Summer, 1996

We had to haul water for the first six months we lived in Haines, because the city's water main construction program was several months behind schedule. Our A-frame's previous owner had moved out and taken the wood stove, the only source of heat, with him when he moved, so for our first several weeks we had to use the kitchen oven for heat. We got our new wood stove in mid-September, just ahead of a freak storm that blanketed the entire countryside with eighteen inches of heavy wet snow. We scavenged drift logs off the beaches for firewood for quite awhile, until the snow got too deep.

Although people said there was no work to be had in Haines, I got a job almost immediately at the Schnabel Lumber Company. I was the talleyman, keeping track of how many board feet of cants (*logs that were squared off on all four sides*) were sawed and bundled each day for eventual shipment to Japan.

Walt Allen, one of the forklift drivers, knew we were desperate for firewood that first winter, so every other day or so he would have an "accident" and break a "smalltop" (*a log that's under six inches diameter on the butt and of very little commercial value*) and holler at me "Better get the chainsaw and clean that mess up. Maybe buck it up and throw it in the back of your pickup and get it out of here." He kept us in firewood all through that first winter, and we were really, really grateful.

I applied for a teaching position with the Haines Borough School District and got hired as the junior high math teacher for the following school year. I fished Bristol Bay for two more summers, and then sold my Bristol Bay boat and bought a local fishing boat so I could fish in Lynn Canal and be closer to home. Little by little we finished the A-frame, and then added on to it, and added on to it again, ... and again, ... and again. The last time I counted, we've added on to the A-frame twelve times, plus a shop building in the back yard. I've done much of the work myself, but we did manage to get Aleta a new "store-bought" kitchen several years after we moved to Haines.

We'd better get back to that 1980 logbook entry. A year after we moved back to Southeast our Anchorage friends Ernie and Lenere and sons Wesley and newly added Jeff, decided they also had enough of the big town and moved to Haines. Ernie is a certified A&P (*airframe and powerplant mechanic*), and planned to open his own aircraft business. A sign advertising "Ernie's Aircraft Service" soon spread across the entire width of one of the few hangars at the Haines Airport, and Ernie was in business.

Ernie and Lenere slowly got established, bought a home, had a couple more children, and got on their feet financially. Of course, during this time Ernie was still able to fly quite a bit. He was always picking up an airplane, or delivering an airplane, or test-hopping an airplane. But he didn't have one of his own, as he'd sold his 170 in Anchorage to help finance their move to Haines.

In late spring of 1980 Ernie and I were visiting one day, and he said "I know where I can get a PA-16 that's in really good condition for $5000. Do you want to go in halves with me on it?"

I had to think seriously about it. I talked it over with Aleta, and we eyeballed our savings account balance very closely, but finally gave Ernie the word -"Go for it." Three weeks later Piper PA-16, N6826 Kilo, arrived in Haines and I was back in the flying mode ... sort of.

My license was endorsed for floatplanes only. Two Six Kilo was a wheel plane, and a taildragger with a very short fuselage and a very narrow landing gear to boot. It was obviously going to be tricky to handle on the ground. It was *almost* a four-place aircraft. That is, it had four seats, but if the gas tanks were full, the little 108 hp Lycoming engine wouldn't lift all that fuel plus four people. The thing was so noisy you couldn't converse during flight. It was as drafty as an old barn and the placard in the baggage compartment said "Maximum Baggage - 15 Pounds."

Two Six Kilo – noisy, cold, under-powered, and tricky to handle, but at least it was an airplane. I could fly again! Haines Airport – September, 1980

All in all 26 Kilo left a lot to be desired, BUT ... it *was* capable of flight, only burned four gallons of fuel per hour, and was dependable. As my mother used to say, "It sure beats a jab in the eye with a sharp carrot."

I spent five hours with Ernie over the next few days, learning 26 Kilo's personality and habits. He had flown it enough to show me the ropes even though he wasn't a CFI. When I felt comfortable in handling the airplane I took it solo and put in several more hours doing stalls, slow flight, maneuvers, and especially take-offs and landings of all types.

After roughly twenty hours of practice I spent an hour with a local CFI who endorsed my logbook as "Recommend for Wheel Rating (SEL)." Shortly after that I flew to Juneau and took and passed my SEL checkride with Wayne Tarbox, the FAA designated examiner.

Don't get the idea that my "practice" in 26 Kilo was drudgery. It's really pretty interesting to practice things like "Turns About a Moose" and "Slow Flight Past a Herd of Mt. Goats," and I guarantee you that it's never boring trying to land a short, narrow geared taildragger in a gusty crosswind, and Haines almost always has a gusty crosswind.

Flying is such a marvelous activity that almost any excuse to get airborne is a good one, and once again I was willing to take anyone anywhere as long as they paid the expenses.

I flew my family to Juneau for shopping trips, even though we couldn't bring much back with us. Dick Buck wanted to spot moose in the Kelsoll Valley. Others wanted to get to Katzaheen Flats, or look for bears along the Chilkat River. John Bruce, one of my fellow ambulance crew volunteers, needed to go to a CPR recertification class in Juneau. A woman wanted to check on her husband and his friends at their moose hunting camp. I made all kinds of trips on other people's gasoline.

Ernie occasionally wanted me to accompany him somewhere as he picked up or delivered an aircraft, and then fly him back home. Yakutat was my favorite destination for these pickup-and-delivery

flights, as we could fly down low over the wide sandy beaches in the area and beach comb. The flight directly to Yakutat is 150 miles, but on one of our ferry flights the weather closed in behind us and we had to fly the coastline all the way back to Haines, a distance of 285 miles.

Two Six Kilo in front of Fairweather Glacier, on a ferry trip to Yakutat with Ernie Walker.
Near Yakutat, Alaska – fall, 1981

On another flight we came across a beached whale, and counted 14 brown bears feeding on the carcass.

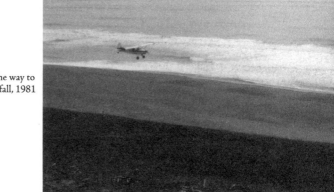

Two Six Kilo beachcombing on the way to Yakutat. Near Yakutat, Alaska – fall, 1981

On still another ferry trip we found a black bear swimming between Sullivan Island and the mainland. We circled low over him, and laughed as he kept rotating so that he always faced the airplane. We finally left because we were afraid we'd wear him out and he'd drown.

We ventured as far north as Tanacross one summer day when we delivered a Cessna 172 and swapped it for a little 90 h.p. Aeronca Champ. On the way back to Haines in the Champ we ran into pretty stiff headwinds, and at one point watched a semi-truck and trailer pass us as we flew above the Haines Highway.

I often visited Skagway, 15 miles north of us, because Haines had no aviation fuel available at that time. We either flew to Skagway for gas, or else refueled from barrels with a hand pump and a chamois filter. Refueling out of a barrel is a two-man operation, so we usually preferred to zip over to Skagway for gas. There's a note in my logbook reminding me that avgas was $1.62/gal in the summer of 1982.

I flew to Whitehorse, capital of the Yukon Territory, just for the fun of it. Those were my first IFR flights in Southeast. IFR officially means "instrument flight rules," but is often used, tongue in cheek, to mean "I follow roads" or "I follow railroads." In this case, I could fly over to Skagway and then follow the White Pass Railroad tracks 110 miles right to Whitehorse. The flight to Whitehorse goes through the Lakes District of BC/Yukon, and is some of the prettiest country around. These big lakes are actually the headwaters of the mighty Yukon River that eventually flows 2000 miles to the Bering Sea.

We tried to visit Sitka periodically, but sometimes had to turn back because of fog or low ceilings. Sitka's runway had been extended to 6,000 feet, and Alaska Airlines was providing daily jet service. Since we had friends and relatives living there, Aleta and I really enjoyed an occasional trip to our old "home town." I enjoy going back to Sitka even today, and it's been over 40 years since we moved from there. Our relatives have all moved away, but we still have a number of good friends living there.

Two Six Kilo was a fun little airplane to fly, but it did have its quirks and idiosyncrasies. Its radio would transmit, but not receive unless the throttle was about half open. The engine had to be turning over above 1500 rpm in order to hear messages. Most of the airports I flew into were uncontrolled, so radio communications weren't a problem. Occasionally I would forget to keep 26 Kilo revved up when leaving Juneau, so I could tell the control tower I was ready to taxi or take off, but couldn't hear their response. I'm sure they got a little impatient with me at times.

I remember providing the tower folks in Juneau with some amusement on one occasion. A sudden storm front blew in from the southwest, with winds gusting over 50 mph. I was ready to depart for Haines, and I knew that I could outdistance the storm front and make it home and land before the winds picked up there. However, I had to taxi 26 Kilo from the transient parking area to the main runway intersection, a distance of probably 300 yards, in a direct howling crosswind.

By holding full left aileron and full right rudder, I could just barely manage to taxi in a straight line, but every time a slightly stronger gust hit me, it would turn the airplane far enough into the wind that I couldn't bring it back again. In order to get back on course for the main intersection, I'd have to continue on around and do a full 360 degree left turn, so my "taxi to the active" consisted of a dozen or more full circles. After the third or fourth complete circle the tower asked if I was OK, and I assured them that I would eventually get to the active runway. The man in the tower responded with "Yeah, I have days when I just go around in circles, too." When I finally asked for takeoff clearance I could hear the tower personnel chuckling in the background.

# Chapter Nine
## A "NEW" AIRPLANE

Two Six Kilo was a good airplane in lots of ways, but in other ways she came up pretty short. It was fine, other than being touchy to handle, noisy, drafty, crowded, overweight and underpowered, so in the summer of '83 Ernie and I sent her on to a new home. We replaced her with one of the nicest aircraft ever built, at least to my way of thinking.

Cessna 170B, N2599C, was all metal, had a stock 145 h.p. engine, but also had a STOL kit consisting of droop wing tips, new leading edge cuffs, flap seals, and beefed-up landing gear with big wheels. Everything about 99 Charlie was dignified, and she behaved herself like a lady. I fell in love with her during the first 10 minutes of flight, and feel the same way about her today, almost 25 years later, even though she's been out of my hands for ages.

Nine Nine Charlie, a Cessna 170B with STOL kit and heavy landing gear, was my all-time favorite airplane. Haines, Alaska – July, 1983

Even though 99 Charlie had almost 50% more horsepower than 26 Kilo, she was much quieter, and much warmer. Visibility was vastly improved, as was cruise speed, and she could handle much more cargo. In addition, control response was smoother and more stable, and she had a radio that was dependable at idle power.

Nine Nine Charlie had huge flaps, wide gear and big tires. She handled really well on the ground, and was equipped for off-runway landings. That meant she could land on the Katzaheen Flats, or at Endicott River or over on the extensive sandy ocean beaches south of Yakutat, although with the STOL kit, the landing area didn't have to be very long. A whole new world of possibilities was opening up.

Charlie and I took to each other right away. You know how sometimes you meet someone and you're on the same wavelength, and almost immediately you're the best of friends? It had been like that with Ernie, and that's how it was with 99 Charlie. It felt like the airplane was an extension of my own self. We just seemed to naturally bond, if it's possible to bond with an inanimate object. I flew her every chance I got.

For the next few months the "remarks" section of my logbook contains entries such as "Family to McDonald's (*Juneau*) for lunch," "Ron Smith - 15 goats, 4 moose, 2 bears," "Family to see Carolyn K.," "Black bear hunt at Glacier Point," "Touch-and-gos on Katzaheen Flats beach," "Set wolverine trap at Katzaheen River," "Rabbit hunt at Turtle Rock," "Night flight, full moon on snow, beautiful!," "Dick Jackson to EMT Instructor class," and "Surprise anniversary dinner in Juneau."

Nine Nine Charlie, our newly purchased Cessna 170B, tied down in front of Ernie's Aircraft Service hangar. Haines, Alaska – Spring, 1983

# Chapter Ten
## A PRETTY SLICK LANDING

By now I'd accumulated around 400 hours, and was really enjoying flying. I had confidence in the airplane and confidence in myself. I guess that's why it was time for another lesson.

Ernie and I were talking about hunting one cold winter day just before my school's Christmas break, and when I expressed the desire to get a wolverine pelt, he responded "Why don't you take 99 Charlie, go over to the Katzaheen, and set some wolverine traps along the river?"

"Nah," I said. "99 Charlie doesn't have skis, so I'd have to land out on the flats and then hike up river on snow shoes 4 or 5 miles, and then the same distance back, The days are too short for that." I coveted a wolverine pelt, but I didn't want one that bad.

"You don't have to land out on the flats," he said. "Fly up the valley and land on the river. The wind has blown all the snow off the river ice, so you can land on wheels. It's been really cold for the past month, so the ice will hold you easy. Just make sure you land on clear, solid ice, and not on that white lacy looking stuff. You can probably land right next to where you want to set your traps. The engine won't be shut off long enough to cool down much at all, so you won't have any trouble re-starting."

The whole idea sounded pretty intriguing to me. My trapping experiences had actually been limited to trapping mice on the front porch of our house, so I went home and read up on wolverine sets, baits, scents, etc., prepped a few borrowed traps and collected the rest of my gear, and a couple of days later went out to the airport, preheated 99 Charlie, and was soon winging over town headed for the Katzaheen Flats.

I crossed Lynn Canal and came down low over the flats, 100 feet or so, then flew up the river two or three miles. I soon came to a bend in the ice-covered river and could see animal tracks of some kind in the snow along the riverbank. It looked like a good enough spot to me, so I did a couple of wide shallow circles over the river to look over my intended landing area. The river was probably close to a hundred yards wide, and the patch of ice I was eyeballing was several hundred feet long, and looked uniformly smooth, hard, and clear.

I did one more turn, dropped full flaps and applied carburetor heat, kept a little power, and got set up to land into a mild crosswind. I came in as slow as possible, cut power just before 99 Charlie touched down, dumped the flaps as soon as the wheels hit, ... and touched the brakes to slow down, and ... Oops!

Oh my! Charlie slewed to the left ... and then to the right ... and then to the left again, farther, and farther still ... good grief, we're sliding broadside ... now we're going backwards ... now we're on around in a complete circle! ... now another circle, faster this time!! The third time around we're almost spinning like a top. Whoa!!!

She finally came to a stop, completely backwards, pointing back toward the spot where I had just touched down. I took a minute to get my heart swallowed and beating again, and then shut Charlie down, gingerly climbed out of the airplane while hanging on to the wing strut, and collected my little backpack and rifle from the back seat. I took two or three steps away from the airplane ... and fell flat on my back! My feet went up in the air, the rifle tossed one way and backpack the other, and I hit so hard that I saw stars for a second. The wind had not only blown the snow off the river, it had polished that ice to a mirror finish so slick and smooth that nothing could stand up on it.

I ended up crawling on all fours over to the bank, where I could finally stand up in the snow. I figured as long as I was here I might as well go ahead and make a set for wolverine, but I knew I wasn't going to attempt another river landing that day. The first one ended up with almost no damage done (*The fall broke the scope on my rifle*), but there were no guarantees that subsequent attempts would be as successful, and I definitely did not want to bend the airplane. After I finished making a cubby set and baiting it I went back to the airplane (*yep, I had to crawl*), started it up, and took off right from where it sat. I wasn't going to risk taxiing on that glare ice again.

I checked the set from the air for the next several days, and towards the end of Christmas break landed again, very carefully, without applying brakes, and picked up the trap. The only thing I got out of it was a little flying time ... and another lesson from the University of Extreme Experiences. And you know something else? I *still* don't have a wolverine pelt.

Nine Nine Charlie on Davidson Lake, at the base of Davidson Glacier. This ice-landing on wheels turned out a lot better than the one I made on the Katzaheen River.
Near Haines, Alaska – December, 1983

Nick Wood, a young family man, moved to Haines and went to work as a mechanic for Ernie's Aircraft Service. He owned a Piper J3 Cub, and regularly spent his lunch hour practicing. He would shoot touch-and-gos, or practice short-field landings, or maximum performance takeoffs. He loved to fly his Cub.

One calm winter day he invited a friend of his to go flying with him during his lunch break. Nick attempted a maximum performance takeoff, and apparently didn't take into account the additional weight of his passenger. The J3 stalled and dove straight down into the ground.

I was among the ambulance crew volunteers that responded. Nick died very soon after being extricated from the wreckage. His friend died shortly after being medevaced to Seattle.

The NTSB Accident Investigation Report (2) states:

ACCORDING TO A WITNESS THE AIRCRAFT MADE AN INTERSECTION TAKEOFF AND IMMEDIATELY STARTED AN ALMOST VERTICAL CLIMB. AT ABOUT 300 FT. ABOVE GROUND LEVEL THE AIRCRAFT

WINGED OVER TO THE LEFT AND DOVE INTO THE GROUND 100 FT. FROM THE RUNWAY CENTER AND NEAR THE UPWIND END. THE HORIZONTAL STABILIZER TRIM WAS FOUND IN A SLIGHTLY NOSE UP POSITION. NO EVIDENCE OF ANY FAILURE OR MALFUNCTION OF THE AIRCRAFT WAS NOTED DURING THE INVESTIGATION. A GROSS EXTERNAL AUTOPSY OF THE PILOT DISCLOSED NO EVIDENCE OF PRE-IMPACT IMPAIRMENT OF HIS ABILITY TO OPERATE THE AIRCRAFT.

The National Transportation Safety Board determines the probable cause(s) of this accident as follows:

AIRSPEED .. NOT MAINTAINED .. PILOT IN COMMAND

STALL .. INADVERTENT .. PILOT IN COMMAND
Contributing Factors
CLIMB .. EXCESSIVE .. PILOT IN COMMAND

# Chapter Eleven
## NIGHT FLIGHTS

Nine Nine Charlie also opened up the world of night flying to me. In midwinter Haines has six hours of daylight, almost to the minute. It gets light around 9 a.m. and by 3 p.m. it's dark again. I was busy at school from at least 8 a.m. until 4 p.m. Monday through Friday, so that eliminated daylight flying time during the week. One clear winter night as I looked out our living room picture window I realized I could see my neighbor's house across the road almost as well by the light of the moon as I could during the day, so I thought to myself "Why not?"

The State had recently installed radio-operated airport lights in Haines, so all any incoming pilot had to do was rapidly click his transmitter button three times on the Haines airport frequency and the runway lights came on. Five clicks turned up the runway lights and turned on the approach lights, and seven clicks turned on runway, approach, and rotating beacon lights, all on full bright. The next weekend was a full moon, so I went out to the airport and started shooting touch-and-gos in the late afternoon, and just kept on going around as the sky got darker and darker. Soon it was full dark, but taking off, flying the pattern, and landing certainly presented no problem. Shortly the full moon rose into the clear night sky over the Chilkat Range and bathed the snow-covered landscape in soft light.

Every terrain feature was clearly visible, like flying in daylight on a really overcast day. I flew up the Chilkat Valley just to get away from the lights of Haines and the airport, and found that I could actually spot wildlife moving across the snow-covered valley floor.

The muted throb of 99 Charlie's engine was the only sound. No one else was in the air. There was no static on the radio and no other traffic to worry about. It was almost like being in a different universe. Southeast Alaska is a spectacularly beautiful place under almost any conditions, but from the air, on a crisp, cold winter night with a full moon and a star-studded sky, it's absolutely magic.

After that first experience I made it a habit to fly at night whenever I could.

## Chapter Twelve
## ANOTHER STEP

By now I felt I was becoming a fairly competent pilot. I had logged several hundred hours of seaplane, wheelplane, and taildragger time, and experienced a sudden yearning to take another step in my aviation endeavors. It was still loads of fun to take off and wander around the countryside, looking for game animals, or poking into little valleys just to see what was there, or flying low-level over the ocean beaches, but when I was flying somewhere with a particular destination in mind, I found myself becoming more and more concerned with being precise.

I started really concentrating on making my takeoff runs absolutely straight down the runway centerline. I wanted liftoff to be smooth as silk, and my climb to altitude to be constant and steady. I started holding 99 Charlie's yoke with only my thumb and forefinger, exerting just the tiniest pressures on her control surfaces. I wanted my altimeter to stay glued to my chosen cruise altitude, and my descents and landing patterns to be uniform and flawless. I wanted to be on the ground without feeling the wheels touch down. My goal became making "the perfect flight."

That winter Ernie bought out an FBO (*Fixed Base Operator*) that was going out of business. I don't remember exactly what he particularly wanted from the purchase, but the part that affected me the most was an ATC 610 Instrument Flight Simulator with a complete set of approach plates for Southeast Alaska. Similar in concept to the Link Trainer of WW II fame (*or infamy, as the case may be*), a simulator allows a pilot to "fly" instrument approaches and departures while sitting safely on the ground. It trains pilots to fly the aircraft by watching only the instruments on the panel, with no outside references at all. I "flew" the simulator over eighteen hours that spring.

Looking back on it, I'm not sure I did myself any good, as all I could do was read the accompanying textbook and then attempt to "fly the approach" on the simulator. I probably developed some bad habits that actually hindered me when I eventually flew with an instrument instructor, but I greatly enjoyed the challenge of teaching myself to fly each instrument approach successfully.

I had taken and passed the FAA Commercial Pilot written exam the previous fall, and after a few hours experience on the simulator, I decided to go for an instrument rating. The instrument rating written test is supposedly one of the most difficult written exams in existence, and instrument flying is a fairly difficult practical skill to master. Instrument flight requires concentration and precision, and that's just what I'd been practicing.

Another excellent Jeppesen programmed course, The Instrument Written Exam, got me on my way, and by early spring of 1983 I had passed the written exam, and enrolled with Gold Creek Aviation, a highly acclaimed accelerated flight school in northern California. I signed up for their commercial pilot program, to be followed immediately by their course in instrument flying. Each course would take 10 days, for a total of three weeks. I planned on finishing both courses by the end of June.

Once I actually experienced some of Gold Creek's program I wasn't particularly impressed. The ground instruction consisted of sitting in front of a TV and watching a commercial video program about the topic under discussion, followed by a practice flight on the same subject. If the syllabus called for a 90 minute flight to practice ILS approaches, for instance, then that flight would be exactly 90 minutes - period - no less, but certainly no more. My instructors, apparently assigned on some kind of schedule, seemed to be knowledgeable enough, but they didn't go out of their way to promote discussions, or to find areas of weak understanding, or help clear up questions.

The commercial pilot's course and subsequent check ride were no problem for me, consisting mostly of being able to maneuver a single-engine complex airplane and stay within fairly rigid parameters while doing it. The FAA examiner who gave me my check ride was thorough, but friendly, and did much to put my mind at ease.

However, I had some doubts about the instrument check ride 10 days later, and wanted to do a couple of extra hours of flying, plus schedule some discussion time with an instructor. The answer was "Don't worry, you'll do fine. Besides, the aircraft and the instructors are too tightly scheduled to deviate from the curriculum like that." Their syllabus was chiseled in stone.

I was scheduled to take the instrument flight exam with an FAA Designee Examiner who was also an air taxi operator on the same airport as Gold Creek. I showed up at the appointed time, 9 a.m., and met the examiner just as he was exiting the front door of his office. "Oh," he said. "Listen, I just got a call for a charter flight from a couple of folks who absolutely *have* to get to Sacramento right away.

Just go on in and be comfortable. I won't be gone long at all." He locked the office door behind me, and left.

When he returned *five hours later* I had looked at every magazine in the place, read everything on his walls, and probably lost 10 pounds due to the California sun pouring in through his picture windows. The office temperature must have been 115 degrees, and the anticipation had turned me into a nervous wreck.

"Wow, it's sure hot in here." he exclaimed. "Why didn't you go in the inner office and turn on the air conditioner?"

"Because it's locked up," I said. But I *thought*, "Wait a minute! It's not *my* office! Why did you leave me in here for five hours while you tooled around on a charter?"

Needless to say, I was behind the eight ball already, and did not pass that check ride. I was not pleased with Gold Creek Aviation or myself. I was a pretty disappointed fellow when I arrived back in Alaska a few days later, and further disappointments were still to come.

I still had half the summer left. I had sold my commercial fishing boat and limited entry permit the previous spring, so I still had the time and money to get my IFR certification. Still wanting an instrument rating, I arranged to take further instrument instruction at Capital Aviation in Juneau. I could fly down to Juneau in 99 Charlie, get instruction in Capital's airplane, and then fly back home again. However, I found (*again*) that an aircraft charter takes precedence over pupil instruction every single time. In addition Capital's only instrument instructor was young, cocky, loud-mouthed, profane and late to each of the few lessons I scheduled with him. I dropped that situation in short order, and temporarily gave up the idea of flying IFR.

In the meantime, 99 Charlie had to move over to make room for a stable mate. Ernie had come across a "deal." Three Canadian-registry Cessna 180s were up for sale as a package, and he bought all three of them. He planned to re-register them in the US, spruce up and modify two of them and then resell them. The third one would become ours, again in partnership.

The first, painted a very attractive blue and white and sporting bubble door windows for better visibility, was sold to a young local fisherman, Ray Willard. Ray had a brand new private pilot license, and now a he had a "new" Cessna 180. Between Ernie and myself we got him checked out on taildragger techniques and sent him on his way. He eventually went on to get his commercial, instrument, and multi-engine ratings, and today (*2007*) is type-rated in a couple of multi-engine jets. Ray began his commercial aviation career flying for Haines Airways, a local air taxi. He moved onward and upward to eventually fly for Flying Tiger Airlines, and is presently flying a jet air ambulance based out of Anchorage.

The second 180, a sporty red and black, eventually went to another fisherman living in Kodiak. I flew this one, 3494 Yankee, to Skagway one day when the south wind was blowing so hard that I couldn't get the tail to stay down when I landed. A couple of helpful bystanders came over and hung onto the struts until I could maneuver off the runway out of the wind and into the lee of one of the airport buildings. When I took off again awhile later, it seemed I was airborne before I had traveled the length of the airplane.

The third plane, mostly white with orange and black trim, was re-registered as 180 WA - the "180" because the aircraft was a Cessna 180, and the "WA" (*Whiskey Alpha, in airplane talk*) stood for Walker & Adkins.

Originally registered in Canada (C-GONY), 180 Whiskey Alpha was part of a three-plane sale. Ernie Walker sold two, kept this one, and I bought half interest in it. Haines, Alaska – March, 1984

I enjoyed flying Whiskey Alpha. It was fun, and fast, and certainly required a higher level of pilot skill and technical expertise than 99 Charley, but although the 180 could carry a bigger load farther and faster, 99 Charley could fly slower and get into shorter places. Charley remained my favorite airplane.

Ernie had another deal cooking about this time, too. In 1978 President Jimmy Carter had signed a bill de-regulating U.S. airlines.

In a nutshell, that law meant that any Tom, Dick or Harriet with an airplane could attempt to start his or her own airline or air taxi service. Ernie and another local pilot, Reggie Radliffe, were contemplating starting their very own airline. It was to be called Haines Airways.

Haines was served by two small airlines at the time, and many local folks thought they both lacked something. Ernie and Reggie thought they lacked competition, so during the fall of 1984 they started the involved and complicated process of obtaining a Part 135 Air Taxi Certificate.

In the spring of '85, when it looked like they were going to be successful, Ernie told me about their plans to start Haines Airways and said "We're going to need at least two pilots to start with this summer, and if the thing is successful, we'll always need extra pilots each summer. If you had your instrument rating, you could have a summer job flying for us every season." *(Air taxi pilots are required by the FAA to have both commercial and instrument ratings, even though they rarely fly IFR in Southeast Alaska.)*

Aha! Fresh inspiration! Fresh motivation! I started searching through the latest issue of *Trade-A-Plane*™, and made a list of several schools offering accelerated instrument ratings. Needless to say, Gold Coast Aviation was *not* on my list! I called several, outlining my desire for an instrument rating, and describing my past experiences. Each one essentially told me the same thing - "We can get you through the instrument check ride." Then I called NorthAire, an accelerated flight school in Prescott, Arizona.

As with the others, I outlined my flying experience and my Gold Coast disaster, and the very friendly lady who answered my call responded with "Just a minute. I'll get you some names and phone numbers of people who have had problems with other programs, and then come here and been successful. Call some of them, and then call me back." Well, that was a different response.

I called some of the references she gave me, and got nothing but glowing reports, so I called her back and made arrangements to take their accelerated Instrument Rating Course, followed by a Certified Flight Instructor Course, starting right after the Haines school summer vacation began.

When I stepped off an Alaska Airlines jet in Phoenix on May 29, 1985, an IFR-equipped NorthAire Cessna 172 was waiting to fly me to Prescott. The pilot, Rob Wadleigh, was to be my primary instrument instructor. "You're here to learn to fly instruments, so let's fly instruments." he said, and had me under the hood by the time we cleared the Phoenix Airport terminal control zone. During the next five days we logged over 20 hours of hood and simulator time, plus several hours a day of ground instruction and discussion time. Rob was incredibly patient, and always available for me. He acted like the most important thing in his world was to get me through this course successfully.

Rob put me through a "rehearsal" IFR check ride on June 4, and scheduled my official check ride for the next day with Jim Morrison, the resident FAA Examiner. The FAA had a resident examiner there because Prescott is the home of NorthAire *and* Embry-Riddle University, the largest aviation university in the world, so someone needed a checkride almost every day.

The next morning Jim put me at ease immediately, telling me that he knew exactly what maneuvers, approaches, and departures Rob and I had practiced the day before, and we were going to do exactly the same thing and in exactly the same order again today. After each successful operation he would mutter a "yes," or "good," or "alright" under his breath, but just loud enough that I could hear. My confidence soared by the minute and my final approach was, according to Jim, "Perfect!" I was an instrument-rated commercial pilot at last.

Six days later I took the CFI check ride, which was actually pretty anticlimactic. The flight was essentially the same as the commercial checkride, with the added tasks of flying from the right seat, and explaining each maneuver to the "student" (*in this case, Jim Morrison again*). After that there was an oral exam on teaching techniques, but since I had BS and MA degrees in the field of education, plus 21 years of classroom experience, the oral exam seemed pretty elementary.

A few days later I was back in Alaska, sitting in Haines Airways' Piper Cherokee Six, N4181W, and going through a Part 135 orientation flight. Every newly hired air taxi pilot has to receive a check ride from the company's chief pilot. Reggie put me through route familiarization, landings, commercial maneuvers, emergency procedures, radio navigation exercises, plus a review of the company's standard operating procedures.

This was followed up by a successful FAA Part 135 (Air Taxi) check ride with Joe Sapp, the new resident FAA examiner in Juneau. I was all set and ready to go. I could fly commercially and get paid for it, and I could instruct student pilots and charge for it. Now people were paying me to fly.

# Chapter Thirteen
## AIR TAXI

I'd better tell you a little bit about air taxis. An air taxi is an airline operating small aircraft, single or twin-engine, that are normally capable of holding anywhere from two to a dozen passengers. Popular aircraft for air taxi services are single engine Cessna 180s, 182s, 185s, 206s, 208s and the turbine powered Caravan, all high-wing airplanes. Piper's contribution includes the high-wing Super Cub, and the low-winged Indian series - the Warrior, Cherokee, and Cherokee Six, Seneca, and similar models such as the Saratoga and the Lance, plus the 10 passenger twin-engine Chieftain. A few Beech aircraft are occasionally found (*but very rarely the V-tailed Bonanza*), and the more exotic "bushplanes," deHavilland Beavers and Otters, and the Nordyne Norseman are represented as well.

In upper Southeast Alaska, the majority of the air taxi aircraft are either Cherokees or Cessna 180-185s or 206-208s. The specifications for all are very similar. Powered by 300 horsepower air-cooled engines, they all cruise at 145-160 mph. They have a useful load of 1,500-1,600 pounds, have a service ceiling of around 17,000 feet, and require a minimum airport length of approximately 2,000 feet. The majority of my air taxi time was logged in a Cherokee Six.

Air taxi aircraft are available for charter, that is, to take a specific party to a particular destination, hence the "taxi" part. They may also have regularly scheduled flights. Sometimes they're also available for instruction and/or rental. However, the fact that the aircraft are small doesn't necessarily mean that the airline itself is small. One of the air taxis in Southeast Alaska owns, operates, and maintains a fleet of over forty aircraft, although the average air taxi fleet size is probably between five and 10. All air taxi operations are certified and supervised by the FAA under Part 135 of the FAA Regulations. That's why it's a "Part 135 Operation." The big airlines, carrying from 20 to 400 or more passengers on a plane, are certified under a different set of regulations, and are referred to as a "Part 121 Operation," and private or general aviation is governed under a third set of regulations, "Part 91."

Many places have air taxi operations, but they're not always well known. For instance the Pacific Northwest has a fairly large number of air taxi operators, but an abundance of good highways and larger cities with jet service relegates air taxis to a minor role in public transportation services. The general public isn't always aware of the services their local air taxis provide.

However, in Alaska, throughout much of British Columbia, and all across northern Canada, air taxis are a basic necessity of modern life. This is especially true in more remote areas. These air taxis carry mail, fuel, groceries and other freight, plus passengers. They are often called into service as air ambulances for medevacs. Sometimes they come once a week, sometimes they come once a day, or maybe several times a day, weather permitting. In a few places they only come on request, and they may be on wheels for airport/airstrip landings, or on floats in coastal areas, or on skis during winter operations, but no matter what their schedule or how they're equipped, they provide a vital service to the residents of outlying communities, logging camps, canneries and mining sites.

Air taxis in most remote areas operate by VFR flight rules only. In other words, they don't fly in clouds, and they won't get you to your destination "regardless of the weather." They fly only when they can see the surrounding terrain. The majority of the landing areas are not equipped for instrument approaches, so air taxi aircraft are usually not equipped with the instruments required for IFR operations either.

*The advent of new GPS and Capstone navigational systems are slowly changing this "VFR only" concept, and causing the FAA to rethink minimum altitude and visibility requirements for small aircraft. Both systems are still very expensive, but as costs come down, more and more air taxis will be equipped for instrument flight.*

This was the kind of operation Ernie and Reggie were proposing. In spring of 1985 their air taxi application was approved, and Haines Airways began service in northern Southeast Alaska. At first, the aircraft, their only aircraft, a Piper Cherokee Six N4181W, operated on a strictly "as-needed" basis. When someone wanted to go to Juneau, 81 Whiskey took them down, often deadheading back to pick up another Juneau-bound party. If someone wanted to come to Haines from Juneau, 81 Whiskey would deadhead down to Juneau and pick them up. It was a very inefficient way to run a business.

They soon added a second plane, a four-place Piper Cherokee 180D, N5170 Lima, which I had purchased for the express purpose of leasing to their company. Having two aircraft enabled the company to go from operating on a charter basis only, to being able to offer scheduled flights to and from Juneau.

The author with 70 Lima, a Piper Cherokee 180D. I bought Lima, nicknamed "The Bean", in April, 1985 with the purpose of leasing it to Haines Airways. It was the company's second aircraft. The company eventually purchased it from me. Haines, Alaska – Summer, 1986

It was still touch-and-go for the first few months, and Haines Airways would probably have lasted less than one summer if it hadn't been for two things - the U.S. Mail and the tourism business.

Each scheduled airline serving an Alaska town gets to carry its fair share of the mail. If there are two airlines, they each get half. If there are three, they each get one third. "Flying the mail" was a lucrative part of Haines Airways business right from the start. During those years every mailbox in town got a Sears catalog, a J.C. Penney catalog, and a Montgomery Ward catalog. Since the Post Office paid for mail delivery by the pound, the weight of those catalog-laden mail flights alone was almost enough to put an airline in the black.

"Walk-up" tourist business was, and still is, brisk during Alaska's short summer season. Glacier Bay tours, icecap tours and general flightseeing made up a big part of that first summer's receipts.

Haines Airways survived the first few months and continued to grow. After a couple of years there was a downtown office in Haines, a ticket counter and freight room at Juneau International Airport, and part-time agents in Skagway, Hoonah, Kake and Gustavus, as well as a big new maintenance hangar at the Haines airport. Several years later it had a fleet of eight aircraft, numerous pilots and a sterling reputation.

I flew the rest of that first summer, and every summer after that, for the next 12 years. I would finish the school year at Haines Junior

High, and often have a flight for Haines Airways the same afternoon I checked out of school. One logbook entry reads "checked out of school at 2:30 p.m. First flight at 5:30 p.m."

In fact, for several of Haines Airways' early years, I would fly a trip in the afternoons after school was out for the day. In April and May there is plenty of daylight in the evenings for a round trip to Juneau or a Glacier Bay tour. In the summer I would fly six days a week (*I always had Sundays off*) until the day school started again in the fall.

Air taxi pilots are legally limited to eight hours of flight time and 14 hours of duty time in any one day, but occasionally this would get stretched a little. One of my biggest and most tiring days involved an early morning round trip to Juneau, and then five straight back-to-back Glacier Bay tours out of Skagway, each 90 minutes long. That amounted to over nine hours of almost non-stop flying, breaking only to fuel the airplane and wolf down one of SkagAir's pilot lunches.

Since I was a summer-hire, the pilots who flew year round had pretty well established their routines and preferences for flights and flight schedules, so I had to take what was left ... and I loved what was left. I would usually have either the 6 a.m. scheduled flight to Juneau, or a 5:30 a.m. charter to Gustavus to catch the daily Glacier Bay day tour boat, and then on to Juneau. Either one of those might be followed by a flight from Juneau to Hoonah, or possibly Kake, or directly back to Haines. Then I would get many of the charters and/or Glacier Bay tours during the day. Alaska Nature Tours and FlyCruise operations usually involved all the pilots. I was always doing something different, and a lot of what I did involved flying around and looking at scenery or wildlife. It was really a tough job, but someone had to do it.

Before I leave the description of air taxis, I should add one more note. Aviation authors often wax eloquent about the smells connected with airplanes. They write ecstatically of the "smell of leather seats," and the "intoxicating tang of aviation fuel," and in older books "the heady scent of dope and castor oil."

Well, an air taxi airplane often has its own set of smells too. In addition to those mentioned, we might add the smell of dog doo, from the Texan in cowboy boots who stepped in a pile just before he boarded your aircraft, and has now cleaned his boots on your rear carpet.

The air taxi airplane often has the smell of fish, from that silver salmon that escaped unnoticed from a broken fish box two days ago and slid out of sight under a seat.

It smells of fish meal from that charter you had last week when you took 30 fifty-pound bags of fish food into Taku Hatchery and had to unload them yourself when nobody showed up at the airstrip. Then just as you were ready to depart, a pickup truck came roaring down to the runway. The driver tells you he has a bad back, and asks if you would you please load those fifty-pound bags onto his truck?

The air taxi sometimes smells of vomit, because the inebriated passenger couldn't find the airsick bag in the seat pocket right in front of him.

It smells of unwashed bodies because the party of five that you just picked up in Dry Bay had been 10 days in solid rain on their river float trip and they had lived and slept in their rain gear, and were really looking forward to get back to Haines for a shower. Brother ... !!! *They* were looking forward to showers??? I could still smell unwashed bodies for days afterward.

It smells of a dirty baby diaper that a young mother changed in midair. She couldn't figure out what to do with it, so she stuffed it in a seat pocket and left it behind. Thanks, mom!

Guess who gets to take care of all those smells, and flies with them if they can't be cleaned up?

# Chapter Fourteen
## GLACIER FLIGHTS (THE CONCEPT)

Haines and Skagway are located between two huge icefields. Glacier Bay National Park is 10 miles to the west and northwest, and the Juneau Icecap is five or six miles to the east and southeast. Lynn Canal, the longest fjord in North America, divides the two icefields. Haines and Skagway are located at the northern end of Lynn Canal, and Juneau, 75 miles south, is at the southern end. Haines and Skagway are the only communities in northern Southeast Alaska that are highway-accessible, and Juneau is the state capital.

For these two reasons, plus the fact that Skagway and Juneau, and to a lesser extent Haines, are popular cruise ship destinations, the area gets hundreds of thousands of tourists every summer. Skagway often logs in more than nine hundred thousand visitors during their four month summer season. Lots of these visitors want to see the glaciers and icefields, and small aircraft offer the easiest, least expensive, and most comfortable way.

Haines Airways, Skagway Air, and LAB Flying Service all offered Glacier Bay tours (GBTs), hour or hour-and-a-half long sightseeing trips over a fairly standard route for a set price. Of course, clients could also charter a longer Glacier Bay flight at a set hourly rate if they so desired.

Another icefield sightseeing venture was sponsored by one of the cruise ship companies in conjunction with Skagway Air Service. A cruise ship would dock in Skagway in the morning, disembark passengers for a day of tourism activities, and return to Juneau empty.

In the evening the passengers would be loaded aboard small aircraft and flown back to Juneau via the Juneau Icecap, weather permitting, and then bussed from the airport to their waiting ship. The only problem, and one that helped get Haines Airways solvent, was that SkagAir usually didn't have enough aircraft of their own to handle all the "FlyCruise" passengers, and would call on other local air taxis for help. SkagAir got a flat rate per passenger for these tours, paid their "helpers" well, and always called HainesAir first when they needed extra planes.

There would sometimes be as many as 35 aircraft involved, from seven or eight different companies. It wasn't unusual to see Warriors, Cherokee Sixes, Cessna 182s and 206s, and amphib Beavers all lined up, waiting for the FlyCruise buses to arrive at the Skagway airport.

Haines Airways was also involved with "Nature Tour" flights. Alaska Nature Tours, a Haines company, takes busloads of tourists, accompanied by a trained naturalist, on a variety of nature tours in the Haines area. One of their variations included expanding into the Skagway market and soliciting customers from the many cruise ships that dock in Skagway. The operation was similar to the FlyCruise concept. We would fly to Skagway, pick up passengers, and fly them directly to Haines, a 10-minute flight. The passengers would do their guided nature tour aboard a bus, and return to the airport. We would then take them on a 30-minute flight around the area, looking for wildlife on nearby Murphy Flats, and then up and around the nearby Rainbow and Davidson Glaciers where we often saw mountain goats. The flight would end up back in Skagway. If Haines Airways didn't have sufficient seats to handle the traffic, we would call on SkagAir first for any help we needed. It was a "You scratch my back, and I'll scratch yours" arrangement.

Occasionally we would be called on to do a flight-seeing tour of the Juneau Icecap. These departed from Juneau International Airport, and were called simply "Icecaps." We didn't do these too often because there was an air taxi company and a helicopter company in Juneau that both specialized in Icecap tours. They got the majority of the Icecap tour business.

I never liked Icecaps, mainly because I didn't get up there often enough to learn all the informal reporting points that local Juneau air taxi pilots used on the Icecap, so I was never positive where other aircraft were when they reported their positions. I was always so busy looking for other traffic that I was never really comfortable on an Icecap tour.

## Chapter Fifteen
## GLACIER FLIGHTS (THE REALITY)

Haines Airways' GBTs followed a standard route that took almost exactly one hour. We would depart Haines airport and a few minutes later fly along the face of Rainbow Glacier, a beautiful little hanging glacier five miles south of Haines. Almost immediately we could turn west and fly up the magnificent Davidson Glacier, our gateway to Glacier Bay, to an altitude of 4,000 feet. At Davidson summit we crossed the boundary into Glacier Bay. I always told my passengers when we were approaching the park boundary, and as we crossed it, I'd jerk the control wheel and say "There, did you feel the bump as we crossed the boundary?"

Davidson Glacier, our gateway for aerial tours of Glacier Bay National Park. Near Haines, Alaska – Spring, 1996

From there we descended the Casement Glacier, then crossed Muir Inlet to the Carroll Glacier, a huge fifty-mile-long stretch of ice. After a wide circle over the Carroll's rugged base, we'd then cross back over the ridge into Muir Inlet and make a circling descent down to the base of Muir Glacier. From there we would follow the shoreline at low level from the Muir to the Riggs, make a big circle up around the huge rock and rugged icefalls in its lower reaches, then go right around the corner to the McBride. Another circle low and tight over the McBride to see if it was calving, and then we'd climb all the way up the McBride and out into Tahkeen Valley, followed by a short flight back to Haines, looking for moose, bears and mountain goats along the way.

Glacier Bay has its own common radio frequency, and all pilots in the Bay are supposed to monitor that frequency. Since there might be as many as 10 aircraft in the Bay doing GBTs, each pilot would report over the base and summit of each glacier with their location, altitude and intentions. This made it much easier to keep track of traffic.

The only really popular non-glacial reporting point was a beautiful glacial-blue pond informally and irreverently named "The Tidy Bowl." The Tidy Bowl is centrally located at the elbow in Muir Inlet, and so was a common reporting point for many pilots on GBTs.

For example, I might report "HainesAir 81 Whiskey, Tidy Bowl, 2.5 (*thousands of feet altitude*), for the Carroll (*glacier*)" and later in the flight I would report "81 Whiskey, base of the McBride (*glacier*), 500 feet and climbing for the top." We still had to keep an eye out for other aircraft, because we would occasionally encounter someone who wasn't reporting (*usually a private pilot, or a "tourist" not familiar with local customs*) but the reporting took a lot of the strain out of GBTs.

One day Midge Stokely, our Haines office manager, called me up to the front desk and introduced me to an older couple who wanted to do a GBT. They were from California, although the man spoke with a strong French accent. He was extremely concerned, he said, because his wife was not a good flyer, and he didn't want her to have a bad experience. Would there be turbulence? Would I turn the aircraft too steeply? Would there be winds aloft? He had a thousand questions, which I patiently answered, often addressing the answers to the wife, who was being pretty quiet and seemed rather shy.

It was actually a rare summer day in Southeast. There wasn't a breath of wind, nor a cloud in the sky. It was absolutely perfect for flying, and as I continued to point this out to the couple, I could see that he was gradually deciding to take the "big gamble" and arrange a GBT. He finally decided to go, paid for two tickets, and we set off in the company van for the airport.

I kept up a reassuring patter to the woman, and when we got to the airport I asked her if she wanted to sit up front with me, or in back.

She replied "Oh no, let my husband sit up front with you." Honoring her wishes I got her situated in the back seat of 70 Lima, a four place Piper Cherokee 180, climbed in myself, and then got the husband seat-belted into the right front seat. From where we were parked we could see both the Rainbow and Davidson Glaciers, so I pointed them out, asked if everybody was all set, and turned the key to start 70 Lima.

The engine caught, and to my amazement the husband instantly threw open the door and vomited violently all over the wing! I was stunned, to say the least, but shut the engine down and helped him get out of the airplane *(without stepping in his own vomit)*. We went over to our hangar's outside faucet and got him cleaned up. He sat in the van while I hooked up a hose and washed down the wing, and then got out and came back to the plane. His wife sat quietly in the airplane while all this was going on.

"It must have been what I had for breakfast" he said. "I've been feeling queasy all morning."

OK, back into the airplane, everybody's all set *(except I'm a little leery, now)*, I started Lima ... and he threw the door open and up-chucked again.

I switched the engine off, and turned to his wife ... "What the... ???"

"Get him out of the airplane," she said, calmly taking charge. I got him out, and this time she followed. We repeated the wash-down job, and she took his arm and led him over to the van. "Stay here and relax." she directed, in a very kind tone of voice. "We'll be back in an hour or so."

She turned to me and said "Let's go. I'll sit up in front with you. He'll be OK here."

The two of us got in the airplane, started up, and taxied toward the active runway.

"He was in the RAF during WW II," she explained. "He flew 15 missions over Germany as a tailgunner in a Lancaster bomber. His aircraft was badly damaged on several of those trips, and was finally shot down over Berlin. He was the only survivor, and now almost 40 years later, he still can't stand to get in an airplane. I've gone through this same scenario half a dozen times with him over the years. He gets himself all psyched up, but in the end he just can't do it."

I called base to tell them I was off on a GBT with one, instead of two, and told them where the husband was. The wife and I had a great flight, and she tipped me $40 on our return.

Haines Airways' Piper Cherokee 180D on a Glacier Bay tour.
Glacier Bay National Park – Summer, 1993

Junior high kids are often pretty blasé, but Glacier Bay's immensity did impress one young 12-year-old boy. I had a family of four from somewhere back in the prairie states on a GBT. This was their first trip to Alaska, and they wanted to see *everything* while they were here. We were in a Cherokee Six, 75 Whiskey, and the 12-year old was sitting up front with me. His mom and younger sister were in the middle row, and his dad was alone in the back row, moving from side to side and taking videos out of both sides of the plane.

Seven Five Whiskey had a PA system in it, so I could easily tell passengers about points of interest, and recite impressive facts about Glacier Bay. I told those folks about Davidson Glacier being 2,000 feet thick at its apex, and about the Carroll being five miles wide and fifty miles long, and had something to say about each of the glaciers we flew over.

As we ascended the McBride I zigzagged back and forth across the surface. I wanted to give all of the folks a really good view, but I also needed to gain 3,500 feet of altitude in order to clear the top of the glacier and get into the Tahkeen Valley, and I didn't see the need of punishing the engine with an unnecessary full-power all-out climb.

Just as we reached the summit the boy, a little wide-eyed and very serious, leaned over to me and said, "You know, there's enough ice here to cool all the Pepsi in the *world!*"

Yep.

Usually when we flew to Skagway or Juneau we would fly the beaches, that is, fly up or down Lynn Canal, but on nice days it was enjoyable to go to Skagway via Lutak Inlet and Ferebee Glacier, or to go to/from Juneau via the Icecap. Both routes are very beautiful, but I don't think there is anything in the world that can match Ferebee Glacier when it's illuminated by the golden light of a Southeast sunset.

Joann Ewen, our Juneau station manager and one of my favorite previous junior high students, met me one day at midmorning as I came in the back door of our terminal area with the news that I had an Icecap Tour scheduled to depart in 10 minutes. As I said before, I've never been too enthusiastic about Icecaps, and thought about asking Joann if one of the other pilot's could do it instead. She already knew my feelings, and quickly added, "There's no one else to do it. Mike went on a charter to Sitka 30 minutes ago, and Dave just left for Hoonah and Gustavus."

Well, OK, it's not that big of a deal. It *is* a beautiful summer day, and should be a really scenic flight, so we'll get on with it and just enjoy the whole process. As I was taxiing in I had radioed the FBO to fuel the aircraft I had that day, one of our Cherokee Six's, 36 Romeo, and as I looked back out the door toward our parking area I saw the fuel truck pulling up in front of the airplane.

I walked back out the door so the driver could see me and shouted "Tips and tabs, please." That meant I wanted the two wingtip tanks filled up (*18 gal. apiece*), and I wanted the two main tanks filled only to the 18 gal indicators (*the tabs*), and not clear to the top. The mains held 25 gal. each. He gave me a thumbs up, and mouthed the word "Oil?" and I shook my head "No." I was never comfortable having other people opening my engine compartment. I would much rather do it myself.

I went back inside to meet my passengers, and found a kindly looking older gentleman and an attractive young girl of about fifteen or sixteen. She was his granddaughter, up from the States for a short visit, and he decided that since she was very interested in taking flying lessons back home, he would take her on a sightseeing flight. They seemed like a pair of really nice people with a lot of mutual affection.

I walked them out through the air taxi exit gate and got them situated in 36 Romeo. Grandpa wanted his granddaughter to sit up front with me, and he sat by himself in the second row. I asked if they had any specific destination or locality in mind, and grandpa said "No, it's just such a nice day, let's go up and fly around the glaciers for awhile."

"Alright," I suggested, "why don't we go around to Taku Glacier, fly up it to the Icecap, and then meander over toward Mendenhall Towers and we can come back down the Mendenhall Glacier."

That sounded fine to them, so a few minutes later we had requested a straight-out departure on runway 8, and were climbing out over downtown Juneau, headed south for Taku Inlet. Grandpa was leaning forward and pointing out different local points of interest to the girl, and they were both really enjoying themselves.

We made the east turn into Taku Inlet and I switched from the Juneau tower frequency to the Icecap traffic frequency. Fifteen minutes later we were climbing the face of Taku Glacier headed for the Icecap, and as we climbed I realized that half a dozen or more other aircraft were also doing Icecaps. I should have figured that, on a beautiful day like today. The only problem was that most, if not all, of them did this all the time, and knew exactly where they were and where they were heading. My radio was filled with position reports, only I didn't know the names or locations of many of their reporting points. I knew the major peaks and glacier summits, but on the Icecap there were lots of check points like our Glacier Bay "Tidy Bowl," not marked on any map, and known only to the "in" crowd.

Grandpa was keeping his granddaughter engaged in conversation, so I didn't have to worry about keeping up a dialogue with the passengers. I concentrated on flying the airplane, and had my eyeballs extended double-distance and on swivels, so I could spot all of this meandering traffic.

We worked our way up to the top of Taku glacier and out onto the Icecap. I heard two or three planes reporting at points that I thought were fairly close to our position, but none of them were at our altitude, so things were still OK. Then I heard a radio call, "There's a Cherokee up here, and I don't think he's reporting. He's going north, just past XXXX (*some colloquial name I'd never heard of*), at about 4000 feet. Watch out for him."

Now I knew how "strangers" felt when they ventured into Glacier Bay. It's like playing a game where everybody knows the rules except you.

I could see the Mendenhall Towers not too many miles ahead, several great towering rock pinnacles rising precipitously a thousand feet above the Icecap. As we approached the Towers I heard "29 Poppa, Mendenhall Towers for Taku Summit, 4.5." Two Niner Poppa was coming my way, five hundred feet above me, and in just a few seconds I spotted him, quartering towards me from my right, a big single-engine airplane on floats, probably a deHavilland Beaver.

We were down close to the Icecap, just a few hundred feet above the surface. Grandpa was pointing to something out the left side of the aircraft, and granddaughter was turned to the left and concentrating on what he was saying.

"Two Niner Pop with oncoming low traffic." He saw us. I clicked my radio mike button twice to acknowledge his transmission, and to indicate that I also had him. He was well above us, but as we neared one another I noticed that his shadow on the ice, much larger than he was, was on a direct collision course with us. "That's kind of interesting," I thought. "It's a good thing he's 500 feet above us."

Just about then granddaughter turned back around, looked out the right side, and immediately perceived our "imminent collision" with 29 Poppa's huge shadow. She screamed and instinctively reared backwards away from the "impact." Of course, when she did that her feet hit the rudder pedals and slewed us around into a severe skid, jolting 36 Romeo almost as harshly as if we *had* hit something. That panicked her even more, and caused her grandpa to think she was having some kind of heart attack or seizure. Apparently he never did see the shadow.

By the time I had us back on the straight and level 29 Poppa and his ominous shadow were well past us. Granddaughter had her face covered with her hands, gasping for breath, and wildly sobbing in relief over our "miraculous deliverance" from certain death. Grandpa tried to comfort her as we skirted Mendenhall Towers, descended the Mendenhall Glacier and went on in to land at Juneau. As we taxied in she was still weeping, partly still from fright, and now partly from acute embarrassment.

Grandpa had his arm around her as we entered the air taxi entrance door. The poor girl, red-eyed and tear streaked, looked like we *had* hit 29 Poppa. Joann looked at them, then at me, and said "What in the world ... ???"

"We just had a mid-air collision up on the Icecap," I replied. "I told you I don't like Icecaps."

❖

Juneau International Airport is the only airport in Haines Airways' immediate area of operation that has a control zone and a control tower. A control zone is an imaginary circle with a radius of five miles, drawn around an airport, and may have one or more rectangular extensions extending further. The zone starts at ground level and goes up to an elevation of 3,000 feet above ground level (AGL). Since the airspace is controlled, the VFR minimums in the zone are 1,000 feet ceilings and 3 miles of visibility.

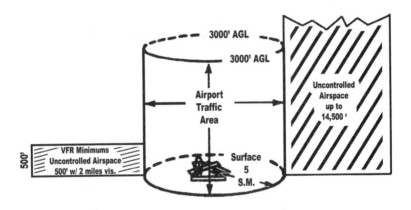

A typical airport control zone.

Aircraft are required to contact the control tower by radio whenever they enter the airport control zone, so the tower can sequence traffic and give landing instructions. After landing, the aircraft is passed off to ground control (*on a separate frequency*) and is directed to its desired destination, which may be a gate, terminal, parking area or fuel dock.

Departing aircraft reverse the process, contacting ground control for taxi instructions, and then are passed off to the tower once they are ready for takeoff. They remain under the tower's control until they leave the control zone. Control zones have very specific rules about aircraft sequencing, spacing, airspeed and separation. For instance, I mentioned previously that a small aircraft is supposed to wait for three minutes after a "heavy" aircraft departs. Another rule is that only one aircraft at a time may be on the active runway.

ATC (*air traffic control, or "tower"*) personnel make sure that landing and departing traffic proceeds in an orderly, dignified and safe manner, even though the folks in the tower often work themselves into a state of nervous prostration to accomplish this. Sometimes, at periods of peak traffic, the whole process must seem to them like trying to herd cats. A few times, when Juneau was really busy, aircraft would be stacked up all over the place just outside the control zone, orbiting and patiently (?) waiting to be sequenced into the landing pattern. ATC, while absolutely necessary at a large and busy airport, also slows down the process, especially at a one-runway airport like Juneau where the same runway is used for both landing and departing traffic.

Sitka and Petersburg both have Flight Service Stations, which offer non-mandatory traffic advisories. All other airports in our area, Haines, Skagway, Hoonah, Gustavus, Kake and Excursion Inlet, were uncontrolled, as was much of the intervening airspace between these places. While "uncontrolled" is really just another way of saying "Y'all be careful now, ya hear?" there is rhyme and reason involved with uncontrolled airports. Each airport has a unique VHF radio frequency assigned to it, called the CTAF (*common traffic advisory frequency*), and all U.S. and Canadian airports have a common traffic pattern for light aircraft.

The common traffic pattern, determined by wind direction, consists of flying with the wind, parallel to the intended landing runway, and off to one side far enough to see the runway clearly. This is done at "pattern altitude," which is standardized for light aircraft at 800 feet above the runway. The pilot continues on this "downwind leg" until he is at a 45 degree angle past the end of his intended runway. He then turns 90 degrees, starts his descent, and flies perpendicular to the runway. This is his "base leg." As he approaches the extended runway centerline, he turns into the wind and lines up with the runway, continuing his descent or "final approach" to the runway.

Sometimes a landing pattern can be flown on either side of an airport. At other airports there may be a terrain feature (*read, mountain*), or some other obstruction that means aircraft can use only one side of the runway. In other words, a pilot may be turning either left or right from his downwind leg to his base leg, depending on which side of the runway he's on. He'll turn the same direction again when turning from base to final. When he enters the landing pattern, he'll specify "left downwind" or "right downwind," so other pilots in the area know his exact location.

When landing at an uncontrolled airport, the pilot tries to enter his downwind leg at a 45-degree angle, and near the downwind end of the runway. His radio announcement on the CTAF would be

"Haines Traffic, 99 Charlie entering right downwind for Runway 8." As he turns onto his base leg he'll announce "99 Charlie, turning right base for 8." As he turns final he'll say "99 Charlie, turning final for 8," and may possibly announce "99 Charlie, short final for 8," especially if he's observed traffic on the ground taxiing for takeoff. After he's landed and cleared the runway his final announcement will be "99 Charley, clear of the active at Haines."

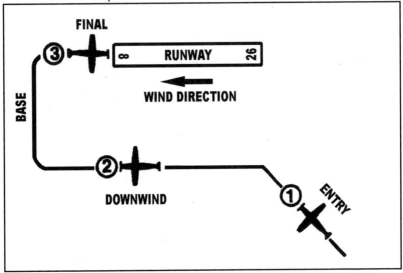

Landing pattern diagram.

OK, now picture this: Skagway Air has a FlyCruise this evening with 103 passengers to transport from Skagway to Juneau, via the Icecap, departing promptly at 7 p.m. This requires 21 airplanes, each carrying five passengers and a pilot. SkagAir has five of its own planes available, so it has arranged with four other carriers to supply 16 more aircraft, all to arrive in Skagway by 6:45 p.m.

Haines Airways dispatches four Cherokee Sixes to Skagway, departing at 6:30. Two of our aircraft are ahead of me, and one is behind. As we go over the town of Haines we can see several aircraft spread out from Battery Point to Taiya Point, all headed for Skagway. As we proceed up Taiya Inlet we begin to space ourselves. All the aircraft have to fly a "right traffic" pattern into Skagway because of the prevailing southerly wind and mountainous terrain to the east.

When the lead aircraft, whoever he is, reaches Burro Creek, two miles off the end of Skagway's single runway, the pilot announces over the CTAF "Skagway traffic, 83 Victor, Burro Creek entering a right downwind for runway 19."

In just a few seconds a similar call from the next airplane ends in "... number two for the runway," followed shortly by " ... number three for the runway," and so on.

Very quickly I'm at Burro Creek, and call "75 Whiskey, Burro Creek, number nine (!) for the runway" There are eight aircraft in the pattern ahead of me, and Number One is still on final and hasn't touched down yet.

Another pilot behind me calls ".. Number Ten ..." just as the first airplane touches down. Now Number One has at least nine airplanes streaming down behind him and he's on the runway that they want to land on. Now what?

He keeps rolling, clear to the end of the runway, and pulls off on the "elephant ear," a turn-around area off to the side of the far south end of the runway, turning his plane so he can see back up the runway, and stopping so he's just barely on the elephant ear but still clear of the runway. He knows he's going to have company *very* shortly. When he looks back he sees Number Two rolling toward him at midfield, and Number Three just touching down at the far end of the runway. Number Four is on short final, and Number Five is turning final.

Number Six sees the congestion at the elephant ear, and radios "Number Six extending downwind so ground traffic can taxi." He's actually not extending very much - he can't because of the terrain, but he is also slowing down to put some space between himself and Five.

Five lands as short as he can, turns around in the middle of the runway and taxis at a good clip back to the terminal and parking area at the far north end of the runway. Four has simultaneously turned around near the south end of the runway and gooses it back towards the terminal, with One, Two and Three pulling out of the elephant ear and rapidly following him. They all swerve off of the active runway and into the parking area, slowing down and parking wherever they can find an open space.

In the meantime, Six is now on short final and touches down shortly after Three clears the runway. Six rolls out to the elephant ear, with the rest of us close behind, and the entire sequence is repeated, only this time we don't have to high-speed backtaxi because Ten was the last aircraft in line. Total elapsed time? Just about four minutes.

Try *that* at a controlled airport ... but it's just business as usual on a busy FlyCruise night in Skagway.

Tourists are a funny lot sometimes. They often can't see what you're trying to point out to them, and on the other hand, they often see things that aren't there.

In the late '70s two families, the Roths and the Allens, homesteaded a few miles south of Haines on Glacier Point (*the Davidson Glacier delta*), an area of approximately three or four square miles. The glacier has been receding for decades now, so most of the delta was covered with good size spruce, alder and willow, but it was interspersed with a number of meadows, especially close to the beach.

The Roths had lived at Glacier Point for quite a few years, and at one point Old John decided he needed a horse, so he barged Buddy, a pure white horse, over from Haines. Several years later Old John died, and shortly thereafter his family decided to leave the isolation of Glacier Point and move into the big city ... Haines!

The Allens weren't that enthusiastic about being out there by themselves, so they decided to move too.

Both families packed their essentials and came across Chilkat Inlet to Haines, abandoning a bunch of stuff they decided they didn't need or couldn't afford to move ... including Buddy, the old white horse. Buddy was left to fend for himself among the moose and bears that frequent Glacier Point. His stable door was left open, and the numerous meadows and abundant beach grass provided him with plenty to eat, so he lived over there all by himself for several years.

Buddy was very useful to us during our Nature Tours. We would descend the face of the Davidson Glacier and then circle the delta at low level, looking for wildlife. Quite often we'd see moose or bears, which thrilled the passengers, but the greatest excitement always came when one of the tourists would spot Buddy, our good old white horse, and shout "Polar bear!"

Katzaheen Flats was another wildlife hotspot on our Nature Tours. After circling Glacier Point we would head towards Skagway, but never without a peek at the Katzaheen. We would almost always see black bear there, too, especially after a couple of the pilots slipped over there one evening and half-buried an old truck tire with a black plywood bear head attached to it.

# Chapter Sixteen
## PEOPLE

People are funny! Have you ever heard that before? Well, an air taxi pilot's main job is to fly people, so things happen with folks who get into airplanes, some pretty funny, and some not so funny.

I was coming into Juneau one summer evening. I had one passenger, a Texan in cowboy boots and a ten-gallon Stetson, in 70 Lima, a four-place Cherokee 140 aptly nicknamed "The Bean" (70 Lima ... as in Lima Bean ... get it?). As we came across Auke Lake I knew that the tower was going to give me a right downwind for runway 26, and as I looked around for other traffic I saw an Alaska Airlines 737 three or four miles to my right, coming in on the other side of the runway for a left downwind for runway 26. The jet was slowed down to 200 knots, and I was going flat out at 115 knots.

I hoped to beat the jet, because if I had to land behind him, the tower would want lots of separation between us (remember wake turbulence? It occurs on landings as well as takeoffs), and I would end up halfway to Taku Arm before the tower would let me turn base and come in to land. So I kept coming full smoke on downwind.

"HainesAir 70 Lima, make immediate right base and short final for landing Runway 26, OR extend your downwind to land number two behind the Alaska jet on left downwind."

I had a wing up into a tight right turn and a diving right base almost instantly, well before the controller had finished speaking. I clicked the mike twice to let the tower know I understood, and did a quick pre-landing checklist while rapidly dropping The Bean out of the sky like a round rock.

The tower had done me a great favor, but now I had a 737 already turning final behind me, and if I wasn't down and off the runway ASAP, that jet was going to have to go around, and I would have a number of people pretty upset with me.

I turned final about a hundred feet above the runway, slowed down drastically by dropping full flaps, and flared out ... and just as I flared, maybe two feet off the ground, the Texan, who had been as quiet as a mouse all through this entirely unorthodox kamikaze landing approach, suddenly grabbed his ten-gallon Stetson off his head, slammed it down on the floor between his feet, and let out a gigantic rebel yell.

"YEEEHAAAHHH!!! I ain't NEVER seen a landin' like this before!!! Whoooppeeee!!!"

Startled out of my wits, the final touchdown was a little less than smooth. In fact, it was a *whole lot* less than smooth, but we were able to turn off at the next intersection, and the Alaska Airlines kerosene queen came smoking in behind us.

One of the things that I didn't particularly like about flying air taxi was that our scheduling frequently made lunchtime a dream instead of a reality. I would often have breakfast at home at 4:30 in the morning, and at 4 in the afternoon (*often even later*) realize that I hadn't had lunch. In fact, occasionally "lunch" wouldn't happen until 7:30 in the evening. I might squeeze in a candy bar, or something like that, during the day, but "mealtime" was frequently just a dream.

The one notable exception would occur whenever I was dispatched to help SkagAir, our "sister" company. If we were doing back-to-back GBTs for Skagway anywhere near mid-day, one of the office girls would be waiting on our return with a selection of deli sandwiches, chips and cold drinks for each pilot. We might only have 10 minutes, in fact there were some times when I finished eating while airborne, but Mike O'Daniel, the congenial owner of Skagway Air, made sure the pilots got something to eat when we were working for him.

May Jane Valentine lived in Juneau at the time, but she had a whole passel of relatives in Haines. She was a originally a Jacquot, descended from one of a pair of French brothers who settled on Kluane Lake in the Yukon Territory during the gold rush days, so she had relatives all over the place, in both Alaska and the Yukon.

She would periodically fly up to Haines, usually on a Friday evening after work, to spend some time with her mother, Edith, who worked in the Haines Post Office. Mary Jane was always conscientious, and frequently brought her mom and other family members a treat from Juneau, something that was exotic and unavailable in a small town like Haines. What was this wonderful and thoughtful present that Mary Jane often brought? It was ... (*want a hint?* ... *think "Golden Arches"*) ... McDonalds!

She would often bring a big sack of Big Macs, Quarter Pounders, Chicken McNuggets and fries, and hold the bag in her lap during the flight, to make sure it didn't spill. I would sit in the pilot's seat, nearly overcome by the smell all those lovely burgers, and salivate so bad it's a wonder Mary Jane didn't think I had rabies. Those were rough flights.

She and her husband retired and moved back to Haines a few years ago, and she and I both presently sit on the Sheldon Museum Board of Trustees. I tease her about those "Big Mac Attacks" and "torturing poor defenseless pilots" every so often. She just grins at me and says "Oh, you!"

❖

When the Golden Arches first came to Juneau lots of people in Haines and Skagway got into the airlift act. Mike Ward, owner of Haines Qwik-Shop, sponsored a couple of 200-burger flights, and always had a huge line waiting for the HainesAir van to make its delivery.

Popular Haines folklore has it that there was actually a fist-fight in the street during one of Skagway's waiting lines, but that could just be one of Haines' urban legends.

Frank Holmes, the Haines Junior High science teacher, used the Golden Arches to his classroom's benefit. "Be good, get your work done, no discipline problems, and we'll have a MacDonald's Fly-In at the end of the quarter," he'd tell his classes, and it proved to be a great incentive. Sometimes we'd have to sweat out the weather, but we never had a Big Mac flight that didn't get through.

HainesAir had an old logger show up one day who chartered a plane to Juneau, had it wait for him while he hiked over to MacDonald's and got a bag full of burgers and fries, and then chartered back to Haines. The burgers probably cost him $4.95, while the charter and down time was closer to $495. Love those Golden Arches.

❖

We flew lots and lots of fishermen, loggers and longshoremen. None of these groups are necessarily known for their close ties with the Women's Christian Temperance Union. We would often find that a group of passengers had spent their waiting time in the airport bar.

FAA regs forbid flying a passenger who is drunk, but we usually figured that if the person could follow us out to the airplane under his own power, they could fly. There were some exceptions, but we soon got to know who might cause trouble and who wouldn't. The belligerent drunk would be "strongly advised" to wait for the next flight, and drink only coffee while he waited. A very few were entrusted to the care of airport security, who in turn passed them off to the Juneau Police Department.

Flying lubricated passengers on good-weather days was fairly easy ... load them in, climb to 5,000 feet in the warm sun, and within 10 minutes all you could hear was snores. Some even had to be shaken awake after we landed and taxied in.

One strict rule applied - No Drinking On The Airplane! If someone broke out a bottle, even a beer, we turned around and went back. Once or twice was all it took for peer pressure to keep the bottles safely tucked away while we were airborne.

Reggie, one of the co-founders of Haines Airways, had a friend. This friend, George, was a 707 captain for Eastern or United or one of those major airlines back on the east coast. George was having difficulties. He was involved in a really messy divorce; his ex-wife was taking him for everything he owned, he was hitting the bottle, and his life was generally a mess.

Reggie, being a good friend, advised George to take a furlough from his airline, bag the whole east coast scene for a few months, come up to Alaska and get back on his feet again.

"Come fly for Haines Airways for the summer," offered Reggie. George thought it over and finally said, "OK."

Almost every pilot in the world starts out in a small aircraft. I suppose there are a few who make their first instructional flight in a Boeing 737, but even the U.S. Air Force starts their pilot training program in Cessna 172s. All big-iron pilots *should* be able to fly small airplanes, but George didn't seem to be able to get it all together.

George was friendly, personable, well dressed (*I can't always say the same for some other air taxi pilots*), good with passengers, and very competent during takeoffs and enroute. But ... George could not land a small plane. He had apparently forgotten his roots.

He flew his landing patterns like he was still in a 707, 1500 feet above the ground, and so far from the runway that he was almost out of sight. His downwind leg would take him five miles past the end of the runway, he would fly his base leg, and then turn final and apparently put his head on autopilot. Once he got lined up with the runway on this long, long, long final approach, he would just sit there and let the airplane fly itself right into the runway. Maybe that's how big multi-jet arrivals are supposed to be, but his landings always looked like a cross between an uncontrolled crash and an aircraft carrier arrest. Passengers began to ask if they had to fly with him.

Reggie worked with him, Ernie worked with him, Rick worked with him, but it was no good. Three weeks after his arrival I flew George to Juneau to catch a flight back to the east coast.

One of my most enjoyable early flights occurred when Dr. Claudia Foster decided to move back to the Lower 48. She and her husband Eric, a ship's engineer with the Alaska State ferry system, had purchased several acres of land on the point at Mud Bay, 10 miles south of Haines on the Chilkat Peninsula. They built a fine custom home, and lived there for several years.

Eric and Claudia were in their mid-thirties, and Claudia's training was in emergency room medicine, so I had gotten to know her through working with her on the Haines Volunteer Ambulance crew. She wanted a job that would allow her more practice in the emergency room, so she and Eric were moving to Seattle, and their beautiful waterfront home was for sale. The problem was, no one in Haines could afford a home like that, and anyone who could afford it would have to travel a long distance to look at it.

So ... Claudia wanted to make a video of their home. She spent several hours videoing the inside and the outside from ground level, and then chartered Haines Airways so she could video it from the air. She and I spent an hour circling at low level and buzzing her place, videoing it from every angle. It was great fun for me, and she and Eric sold the house to the first person who saw the video.

Haines Airways and one of its local competitors were at war. HainesAir had been purchased by Mike and Barbara Shallcross the previous winter, and the older "hometown" air taxi owner apparently figured this would be a good time to eliminate his "newcomer" rivals. He proceeded to initiate a price war.

The ticket price from Haines to Juneau dropped week after week ... $65 ... $60 ... $50. Every time the competition dropped his price, Mike would lower Haines Airways' price to match it.

Fares finally dropped to $35 one-way and $65 round-trip, a price so low that it hardly covered the cost of fuel, much less anything else.

After a few days of this the rival owner came storming into Mike's office and belligerently demanded to know "How much will it cost me to buy you out and get rid of you?"

Mike calmly looked him in the eye and said, "We're not for sale at any price. How much would it cost *me* to buy *you* out?"

"You can't afford to buy me out!" the rival fumed. "Why, I've got over 40 aircraft alone. You'd have to come up with three million dollars."

Mike smiled at him and quietly said "It'll take me two phone calls and an hours' time to have a certified check for you. Do you want to wait, or should I bring it on down to your office?"

The man stared at Mike for a few seconds, then turned and stomped out of the office.

The next day the price war was over, and fares were back up to $70 one-way.

I had Kay Haas as a student in junior high school, and also coached her for two years in the school's rifle club. She was a real sweetheart all through school, so I was glad to see her working in our office one summer. Rick Dunning, one of our full-time pilots, was glad too. Cupid bent his bow, fired his arrow, and the following summer (1986) Rick and Kay were married.

I always started flying early in the morning, but I told the dispatcher on their wedding day that I would fly late also, to cover any other pilots who wanted to go to their wedding.

It turned out to be a *really* busy day. I flew almost continually from 5:30 a.m. until after 9 p.m., and got to the wedding reception just as the bride and groom were leaving. I kissed the bride, shook hands with the groom, grabbed a piece of wedding cake, went home and collapsed in bed.

After all, I had another 5:30 flight in the morning.

*In the summer of 2006 Rick and Kay called me from their home on the east coast where Rick is now a 747 captain. They were returning to Haines to repeat their wedding vows for their 20th anniversary, and wanted to make sure that I was invited, since I had missed their first wedding. I thought that was very thoughtful of them.*

In Haines, each of the air taxi companies provides courtesy van service. Passengers within the townsite area are picked up and delivered, on request, as part of the air taxi's service. Each company has a van driver, and Haines Airways was no exception. The only hitch was that our driver didn't come on duty until 8 a.m., and my first flight was usually at 5:30 or 6 in the morning, so if we had passengers who wanted to be picked up, I had to do it.

One particular morning I had the 6 a.m. scheduled flight to Juneau. This meshed with Alaska Airlines 7:30 departure for Seattle, which was a pretty popular flight with Haines residents. I had one passenger listed, and a pick-up had been requested. I didn't recognize the name of the passenger, but the pickup address was the home of one of the more prominent families in town.

I pulled into their driveway at the pre-arranged pickup time, 5:30, and a very attractive young blonde woman, perhaps in her late twenties, came out the front door to meet me. I greeted her, took her one medium-sized suitcase from her hand, and put it in the back of the van. I then opened the front passenger door and waited for her to get in. Which she did not do. She continued to stand on the sidewalk, 10 feet from the van.

"Is anyone else going with us?" she asked. "Will anyone else be with us in the van?"

"Nope. There will be just two of us in the van, and just two of us in the airplane. You're the only one going this morning."

"Oh. Goodness, I don't know if I should be alone with you in the van or not?"

Hmmmm ... I looked a little closer at her now. She was, as I said, very attractive, and very well dressed. She had on a just-above-the-knee length suit of some kind, a little pillbox hat, and matching high heels and purse. Overkill for an Alaskan air taxi, but she was catching a jet for Seattle, so her mode of dress probably wasn't too far out.

Then I looked more closely at her face, and she gazed back at me with her great big baby blue eyes ... and I could see clear to the back of her head. Oh ... !

Just then the front door opened, and the lady of the house came out in her bathrobe and slippers. "It's alright, Janie, you can go with him. I know this man and he's OK. You can go with him."

"Oh, thank you, Aunt Mabel. I'll see you later. Be sure to write," she said, and climbed in the van.

On the way to the airport Janie told me that she had come up to visit her Aunt Mabel and Uncle Bert two weeks before, and had a *really* nice time, and *really* liked Haines, and had met some *really* nice people, and was *really* glad to be going home. She seemed like a *really* nice young woman, but it was obvious she wasn't *really* very sharp, which of course wasn't her fault. We all have to play the hand we're dealt.

Since she was the only passenger going, I tossed her suitcase in the back seat of the airplane, slid into the pilot's seat, and then politely studied something out the left window while she tried to modestly maneuver herself, her high heels, and her short skirt into the right front seat. It can't be done, so I looked at the left wingtip until I sensed that she was situated.

All the aircraft in our fleet had the right front control wheel removed, with the exception of 36 Romeo, the Cherokee Six we were using this morning. Pilots always fly from the left seat, so it's much easier for both pilots and passengers to get in and out of the front seats with the right-side control wheel removed. However, since 36 Romeo was used occasionally to check out new pilots, it still had the dual control wheels.

We taxied out to the active runway, saw no traffic in the pattern, so I pulled out and firewalled the throttle. A lightly loaded Cherokee accelerates pretty fast, so reaching liftoff speed, 85 mph, happens quickly. The airspeed indicator went right on around ... 40 ... 50 ... 60 ... 70 ...

Just then Janie reached out, and catching me completely off guard, grabbed the wheel in front of her with both hands, pulled it back into her lap so she could get a better look at it, and cooed, "Oooohh, what's this little wheel on *my* side for?"

I instinctively smashed her hands off the yoke, yelled "Keep your hands off the wheel!!!" and pushed forward, but poor old 36 Romeo, just about ready to rotate, had already reared up, nose in the air at an impossibly high angle, and was entering a full-power stall twenty or thirty feet above the runway.

I thought for sure the airplane would fall off on a wing and we'd end up in a big ball of fire just off the runway, but Romeo waffled along, behaving herself like a true lady and staying on the straight and narrow while I walked the rudder, trying to regain control. She sank back toward the runway as the nose came back down. The landing gear thumped back onto the runway, ran along the asphalt for several more seconds, and very shortly we were back under control and showing 85 mph. indicated airspeed.

Takeoff after that was normal, as was our flight to Juneau. Janie kept her face turned away from me, her arms folded in front of her, and looked directly out the right window all the way to Juneau. She was obviously in an outraged pout, and that was just fine with me. I have a hard time being civil to people who attempt to kill me that early in the morning, so I was pretty ticked off myself.

I got out of the airplane at Juneau, grabbed her bag, and headed for the Alaska Airlines counter, leaving her to totter along on her high heels as best she could. I dropped her bag at the end of the ticket line, turned around, and there she was, right behind me.

She smiled and batted her big baby blue eyes at me. "Thanks for a wonderful flight," she said quietly, and held out her hand and palmed me a twenty dollar bill.

Go figure.

The next morning I noticed that 36 Romeo's passenger side control wheel was gone.

The two men, both locals, well known and well liked, took off the evening before the opening day of moose season. Someone saw them fueling the little yellow side-by-side 90 h.p. Aeronca Chief shortly before they departed, asked where they were going, and were told they were going to go spot moose. Then the next day they could hunt, either by boat or by vehicle, depending on where they found moose. They didn't return before dark, so launching a search had to wait until the following morning.

Ed Mackey, the pilot and owner of the airplane, was a low-time pilot (*213 total hrs.*). His passenger, Dan Pardee, had no aviation training at all. They were both in their 30s, large men, in good physical condition. One worked in the timber industry, the other was a commercial fisherman. They had filed no flight plan, and their search for moose could have taken them anywhere in the Chilkat Valley, an area roughly 40 miles long and 15 miles wide. Searchers were looking for a yellow airplane in an area that was full of birch, alder, and vine maple, all decked out in their fall colors - yellow. The search went on for many days, but no trace of the missing plane was found.

Over a year later, during a spring brown bear hunt, a local guide was flying his client up the Chilkat River, and telling the client about the missing airplane. He said "I wouldn't be surprised if it's not down someplace right along here, right along this river bank." He pointed down, and realized he was pointing directly at the tail assembly of the missing plane. The bare metal framework was sticking up above a patch of budding alders, right next to the river.

Ed and Dan had apparently seen a moose along the river, and circled too low and too tight for the little underpowered Chief. It stalled and went straight down into the patch of alders. It was a classic example of one of Alaska's greatest aviation hazards - The Moose Hunter's Stall.

The NTSB Accident Report (3) stated:

DEPARTURE POINT: HAINES, AK

INTENDED DESTINATION : RETURN

LAST ENROUTE STOP: UNKNOWN/NOT REPORTED

TYPE OF ACCIDENT: STALL    PHASE OF OPERATION: IN FLIGHT

OTHER PROBABLE CAUSE(S):
PILOT IN COMMAND - FAILED TO OBTAIN/MAIN-TAIN FLYING SPEED

FACTOR(S): PILOT IN COMMAND - DIVERTED AT-TENTION FROM OPERATION OF AIRCRAFT

MISSING AIRCRAFT LATER RECOVERED - FIRE AF-TER IMPACT

REMARKS- LOOKING FOR MOOSE.

# Chapter Seventeen
## WEATHER, AIR TAXIS, AND SPECIAL VFR

The FAA has established certain "minimums," that is, ceiling and visibility requirements that, for safety's sake, are not supposed to be transgressed. Those minimums are different for controlled airspace and uncontrolled airspace. Since most of Southeast Alaska is uncontrolled airspace, we'll concentrate there for the time being.

The minimums in uncontrolled airspace, roughly defined, are 500 feet ceilings, two miles visibility, and clear of clouds. I suppose it's only natural for people to push the envelope, but Southeast has some pretty unique weather conditions. It's an extremely moist coastal environment, with lots of cold air from glaciers and icefields thrown into the mix, making for some strange weather conditions at times.

Since it's not at all unusual, especially in the summer, to have low ceilings, sometimes with almost unlimited visibility underneath, what is a pilot to do? If the ceiling is 450 feet, and the visibility underneath is 15 miles, should the air taxi pilot say, "Nope, sorry, I can't bust minimums"?

If the conditions on the way to Juneau are 1,000 feet ceilings and 10 miles visibility, except for Berners Bay, where there's a stretch of about two miles across the mouth of the bay where conditions are 400 feet and 10 miles, should the pilot turn around and go back?

Quite often I'd take off for Juneau in the early morning and face layers of fog in the Canal. I might get to Point St. Mary at a thousand feet, and have to drop to 300 feet, or even lower, to cross the mouth of Berners Bay. In May and June there would often be humpback whales breaching along the beach between Point Sherman and Point St. Mary. Whales can get about two thirds of their body length out of the water when they breach, and sometimes I was so low that it seemed like I might run into them as they propelled themselves out of the water.

Occasionally I'd have to detour and circle out towards the middle of Lynn Canal before I could get around, or above, or below a fog bank.

Other times there would be absolutely no way to get around the fog bank, so I'd end up crossing Lynn Canal, usually at low level, to the west side to see if I could follow the beach there, eventually skirting Lincoln Island and Shelter Island, and getting into Juneau that way.

Fog could form anywhere, but in Lynn Canal it's especially likely to form at Berners Bay, around Eagle Beach, and in Auke Bay. Those areas have glaciers coming down off the Icecap, so cool air flows down and hits the warmer moist ocean air and forms fog. My logbook contains series after series of notations reading "500/2" (ceiling/visibility), "500/3," "200/1 fog all day," "JNU closed," "rain and fog," and "turned around twice."

I once spent over an hour circling around above a fogged-in Juneau airport with four passengers. We were in bright sunshine, and I could see both ends of the runway clearly, but the tower was showing visibility less than one mile, so I couldn't even get a Special VFR clearance.

Even when the weather was good it could be bad. There was a stretch in late summer of 1994 of almost two weeks where my logbook entries all say "Ceiling unlimited, visibility 2 miles due to smoke." Forest fires in the Yukon sent thick smoke billowing down into Southeast Alaska, and there were a couple of afternoons when we actually had to quit flying due to low visibility.

Many flights result in the pilot having to make a judgment call. There's no one out there looking over his shoulder, but he knows two things. First, if he busts minimums, screws up and something happens, he's going to be the very first person at the scene of the accident, because he's sitting in the front seat. Second, the FAA investigators are going to find "pilot error" to be the cause of the accident. That means he may not have a pilot's license anymore, presuming he's still alive and still wants one.

Ernie and Reggie were really good about weather flying and safety. Some companies want their pilots to push, push, push. Their motto is "You've *got* to get through!"

Ernie said "If three of you are going somewhere in bad weather and you don't feel comfortable, do a 180 (*turn around*) and get out of there. I don't care if the plane ahead of you and the plane behind you both get through. You're the captain ... if *you're* not comfortable, don't go!" (*As a result of this conversation, I acquired the title of "Cap'n Bob," which has stuck with me for well over twenty years.*) Reggie agreed with Ernie, and that was company policy for the next 12 years. No one ever questioned a pilot's decision to turn around, at least not at Haines Airways.

We always knew what the weather conditions were like at our

home field, and we could always find out what the conditions were at our destination. The problem was, we didn't know what was in between. There's a stretch of 45 miles between Haines and Juneau where there isn't a single living soul. There's no one living in the 90-mile stretch between Haines and Gustavus. This is where pireps (*pilot reports*) come in.

All flight plans in our entire area are filed with the FSS (*flight service station*) in Juneau. We'd call their frequency (*"Juneau Radio"* ... *different from "Juneau Tower" or "Juneau Ground"*) on the radio to file, and often they would request a pirep, especially if no other planes had flown that particular route yet that day. Sometimes if we encountered something unusual we'd call and make an unsolicited pirep. Once a pirep was available, it was passed on to every other pilot flying that route as they filed their flight plan.

Of course, no one filing a pirep ever reported conditions less than 500 feet and two miles. A pilot might be ducking under a cloud layer and at 300 feet for a mile or so, but if you reported that, you were essentially turning yourself in for violating minimums, and someone from the Friendly Aviation Authority would very likely be around shortly to talk to you and your boss.

I was deadheading from Gustavus to Haines one morning. The overcast was varying from 500 to 600 feet, but there was good visibility as I flew along the beach headed for home. I heard someone asking Juneau Radio for a pirep from the St. James Bay area. They responded that they didn't have one yet, so since I was just going past St. James I radioed to give them a pirep.

"Juneau Radio, HainesAir 75 Whiskey with a pirep from St. James Bay. Visibility is at least 10 miles, and the ceiling is an honest 500 feet." They rogered, thanked me, and I flew on home.

Half of the air taxi pilots in the entire area must have been listening to me give that pirep. For the next week I'd meet some pilot in the terminal or at the airport and they'd look at me, laugh, and say "An *honest* 500 feet, eh?" I guess many of those "500 feet ceiling" reports weren't ...

As I explained before, each major airport has a control zone surrounding it, with a control tower to regulate and control the traffic flow. This includes flights that are arriving on an IFR flight plan. All heavy aircraft, commercial or military, will file an IFR flight plan, no matter what the weather. They're given an IFR clearance, they fly under ATC control during their entire flight, approach their destination guided by distinct radio pathways in the sky, and land, providing the ceiling and visibility are above IFR minimums. When on an IFR flight plan, the pilot is assured that no one else is in his block of airspace, including in the airport control zone. If the weather at their destination is good, they will call the control tower to "Cancel IFR - airport in sight," and land by visual references, just like the little planes.

An air taxi pilot can avail himself of somewhat similar consideration. If the airport control zone is below VFR minimums *(1,000 ft. and 3 miles)*, but is still above uncontrolled airspace minimums *(500 ft. and 2 miles)*, a pilot can ask for a "Special VFR clearance." The pilot must stay outside the control zone until the Special VFR clearance is issued by the tower.

When the tower clears the pilot for Special VFR, that means the pilot can now enter the control zone, visually pick his way through the scud, and land, with full assurance that his is the only airplane moving within the control zone.

Why don't the air taxis fly IFR so they can come and go in bad weather like the jets do? Well, here's the situation in our area. I can leave Haines on a VFR flight any time I choose, and follow the beach 65 miles to Juneau at an altitude of 500 feet. As long as I can see two miles along the beach I'm legal. When I reach Juneau I can ask for a Special VFR clearance and land.

If I file IFR *(assuming my airplane is certified and equipped for instrument flight)* from Haines to Juneau, I have to leave when ATC tells me to. I have to climb to at least 8,000 feet in the clouds because FAA rules say I have to be 2,000 feet above the terrain, and our mountains average 6,000 feet high. I have to fly 85 miles, in cloud and following a particular radio beam, to the Sisters Island VOR to get on the Juneau instrument approach, and then fly another beam 20 miles back towards Juneau, descending all the while, carefully staying on the radio beam and at a specified constant rate of descent. Now remember, all of this is taking place in solid cloud. I can't see a thing outside the airplane. When I finally turn onto my IFR final approach, I can only land if the Juneau airport weather is above the published IFR minimums, which are ... you guessed it ... 2000 feet and 2 miles, higher minimums than I would have had if I had just flown down the beach, asked for Special VFR, and saved all that wear and tear on the airplane and on the pilot.

❖

Boyd Hoops and I each flew a Cherokee Six to Juneau one morning. The weather was pretty low in Haines and Lynn Canal, and got lower and lower the closer we got to Juneau. When we got to Auke Bay, Juneau tower told us the field was below minimums and we couldn't land at present, but conditions were improving. We could see that in Auke Bay the fog was almost down to the water level. We both knew that as the morning sun came up the fog would dissipate pretty rapidly, so we decided to orbit for a while. Boyd circled just off Lena Point at about 500 feet, and I moved slightly west and flew around the southeast point of Shelter Island.

After a few minutes Boyd called Juneau Tower. "Juneau Tower, HainesAir 56 November is orbiting Lena Point with a flight of two. We'd like to request Special VFR as soon as conditions permit."

"HainesAir 56 November, Juneau Tower, Roger."

In other words, take a number and wait, but at least when conditions improved a little, we'd be first in line for a Special. In the meantime a Skagway Air pilot came flying into the area, and since he'd been listening on the radio, knew what the form was, so he just picked a spot slightly north of me and circled. Most of the air taxi airplanes have two radios, so the three of us were gabbing on the Lynn Canal CTAF, and monitoring Juneau Tower, waiting for their call that we could have a Special VFR.

A couple of more minutes and an LAB plane out of Hoonah or Gustavus, I was never sure which, came along, saw what was going on, and orbited the southwest point of Shelter Island, just west of me. Almost immediately an Air Excursion plane out of Gustavus showed up, so we had quite a little assembly of circling aircraft just outside the Juneau control zone.

In a few minutes Juneau Tower came on and said "HainesAir 56 November flight, you're cleared into the Juneau control zone Special VFR. Keep each other in sight at all times."

Boyd rogered them, told them we were entering the control zone, and then said over the CTAF frequency "Come on, all you guys. We're cleared for a Special. Don't lose sight of the airplane in front of you." If we had each come in on an individual Special VFR clearance, the last airplane would have had to circle out there for another half hour or more. This way we would all be on the ground as soon as possible.

A few seconds later Juneau Tower queried "56 November, how many did you say were in your flight?"

"Tower, 56 November, Five."

A long pause ... I think it's actually called a long *pregnant* pause.

"FIVE ???"

"Roger," he responded, and immediately added, "We're all inbound in the control zone."

All five of us had quickly lined up and started across Auke Bay, low level and weaving around the patches of fog, playing follow-the-leader. The controller was trying to deal with the fact that he'd just inadvertently cleared an entire fleet into his below-minimums control zone and there was nothing he could do about it. We were all busy keeping each other in sight while we zigzagged around patches of low fog.

In a couple of minutes Boyd sighted the rotating beacon that marks The Cut, a deep notch in the ridge at the west end of Juneau's airport. He went through with what seemed like 50 feet clearance, with the rest of us hot on his tail at close intervals. The last plane in line was on short final as Boyd turned off at the main intersection.

The controller was either on the floor having a nervous breakdown, or else on the floor laughing at the humor of the whole situation. We five laughed about it, too, but no one else ever said a word about our "Special VFR fleet arrival."

Juneau International Airport is located on a large flat delta that borders Gastineau Channel, and is at the foot of Mendenhall Glacier. Cold air from the glacier flowing down and meeting moist air from the channel means that the Juneau airport sometimes has some rapid and drastic weather changes. Rich and I flew two planeloads of travelers down to Juneau early one calm August morning.

The surrounding countryside was bathed in early morning sunshine, but the airport itself, while wide open, showed signs of an impending local weather "occurrence." Thin wispy tendrils of fog hung about all over the Mendenhall valley, draping the airport in gauzy, lacy patterns, and giving sure and certain indications that "something" was going to happen.

Rich and I unloaded our passengers and their baggage, found we had a little free time between flights, and decided to have breakfast in the airport restaurant. We sat by the big plate glass windows that faced the glacier, and by the time we'd finished eating, thick fog had developed, to the point where we could barely see across the street.

"We're here for awhile," we reasoned, "so we might as well have another cup of coffee and relax."

Well, we were the only ones who were relaxed. The Haines office was overrun with tourists who wanted to do GBTs on such a beautiful day. A group of local government officials had to get to Juneau. Fish and Game needed to do an aerial survey of something or other. The phones were ringing off the hook, and Rich and I were drinking coffee while a third of the company's airplanes were fogged in at Juneau.

A Haines Airways Piper PA-32-300 Cherokee Six sits on the ramp in Haines, waiting for the early morning fog to burn off. Haines is clearing, but Juneau is still fogged in.
Haines Airport – Summer, 1995

When we phoned the Haines office to check in, Midge Stokely, the Haines office manager, asked us, told us, begged us, to get to Haines as soon as we could. "Sorry, Midge. No can do ... it's socked in tight here. Absolutely nothing is turning a prop."

An hour or so later I glanced out the window again, and saw the fog on the glacier side of the airport was starting to lift just a tiny bit. It certainly wasn't clear, let's just say there was a little pocket of less dense fog, but we could see through it, and could see a light area that indicated the glow of sunshine higher up on the face of the Mendenhall Glacier.

We walked to the other side of the terminal building, facing the runway, and saw that the pocket included midfield, but both ends still looked pretty foggy. Hmmm.

We went back to our ticket counter and I called upstairs to the tower and talked to the controller. "Our company needs us badly up in Haines. Can we get a Special VFR to depart runway 26 at intersection C, and fly up the Mendenhall?" I asked.

"Let me look." the controller responded. He came back on a minute later and said "It's still pretty marginal, but I guess we could do that."

Three minutes later I was in my airplane and radioing, "Juneau Ground, HainesAir 75 Whiskey, flight of two, taxi 26, request Special VFR, departing to the north."

"Roger, 75 Whiskey, Special VFR is approved. Don't overfly any airport buildings."

Rich and I launched from C intersection, got airborne, immediately turned sharp right over the main intersection, and departed at cartop level across the west parking lot, between the passenger terminal and the air freight building. By the time we reached Mendenhall Lake the fog started to dissipate and we were able to circle up into the bright sunshine. Forty-five minutes after pioneering Juneau's first "West Parking Lot Departure" we touched down in Haines.

A fair number of air taxi flights in Southeast Alaska have to turn around due to weather. Conditions often change rapidly and unexpectedly, there are rarely weather reporting stations between destinations, and the terrain is such that fog can form suddenly in little pockets and valleys.

For example, three of us were finishing up a Nature Tour flight, returning fifteen tour ship clients to Skagway after a Davidson Glacier sightseeing flight under a 5,000 foot overcast. The traffic pattern in Taiya Inlet calls for all incoming and departing traffic to stay to the left, so we were flying close to the mountains, and had to make a dogleg turn about three miles out of Skagway. I was in the lead, and as I rounded the dogleg I was confronted with a totally unexpected wall of pea soup fog that went clear down to the water. I had to make a split-second decision to turn around, or I would have been enveloped in fog, with mountains close by on each side ... *not* a healthy place to be.

The two planes behind me had more warning than I did, so shortly we were all three on our way back to Haines with fifteen nervous passengers who were afraid their ship would leave Skagway without them.

Midge, our office manager, contacted the tour ship and received reassurances that they weren't going to leave their passengers stranded. Since our schedule was shot anyway, we all went and had a pleasant lunch together, and two hours later the fog had dissipated and we delivered our passengers to Skagway under a bright, sunny sky.

The air taxi pilot, relatively new to the area, was flying in heavy fog, trying to follow the beach north up the Chilkat Peninsula. Had he been more familiar with the area, he would have realized that the beach line would take him into a small bay. As the beach turned sharply back under him, he had no choice but to try to climb up through the fog to the clear air above. He couldn't climb steeply enough to clear the terrain, and flew into a tree-covered hillside.

The NTSB Accident Report (4) states:

WHILE ON A VFR FLIGHT FROM SKAGWAY TO JUNEAU, AK, THE PILOT ENCOUNTERED OBSCURING WEATHER CONDITIONS AND REVERSED COURSE. EN ROUTE BACK TO SKAGWAY, HE ENCOUNTERED LOW CEILING, RAIN AND FOG. HE DESCENDED TO FLY UNDER THE WEATHER AND LOST VISUAL REFERENCE AT ABOUT 150 FEET ABOVE A SALTWATER INLET. HE INITIATED A CLIMB IN INSTRUMENT CONDITIONS, BUT THE AIRCRAFT IMPACTED ON A STEEP, WOODED HILLSIDE. THE AIRCRAFT WAS DESTROYED, TWO PASSENGERS WERE KILLED, AND FOUR WERE SERIOUSLY INJURED.

# Chapter Eighteen
## XIP

Yes, I can spell. No, it's not a college fraternity. XIP is the three-letter destination code for Excursion Inlet Packing Company, a large fish processing plant near Gustavus and Glacier Bay, at the mouth of Excursion Inlet. XIP is isolated. There are no roads to it, or even near it. It has a large dock, of course, because fishing boats and tenders come in to unload vast amounts of freshly caught salmon, halibut, and other seafood. All of XIP's product is shipped out by boat, and most of their supplies come in by boat, too, but air taxis are also in and out of there a lot.

There isn't exactly a runway at XIP. Airplanes land on the narrow dirt road that runs through the middle of the cannery buildings and out along the beach. Or maybe the cannery uses the runway as their road ... I guess it depends on how you look at it.

There are three radio-activated flashing blue strobe lights along one edge of the road, operated by clicking the airplane's mike button on the discrete XIP frequency. The purpose of the lights is to warn anyone on the road, usually kids on bikes or four-wheelers, that an airplane is landing. The pilot clicks his mike button, the lights flash on, and kids scatter like chickens ahead of a fox, but as soon as the plane is safely down they're right back out on the road again.

Anyway, in order to land into the prevailing southerly wind, you fly a right downwind leg over Excursion Inlet, make a short base leg and turn to final to line up, more or less, with the road/runway. While on final you dodge to the right around a tall steel radio tower, then slip to the left away from the bunkhouse roof, straighten out, and you'd better touch down on the first few feet of the short runway, which has a slight curve in it. If you land too long, you'll run into the trees at the far end. It's another one of those "Y'all be careful ..." things.

XIP was always a charter destination for Haines Airways. We didn't run a schedule into the cannery, and I don't think any other air taxi did either. But somehow, Libby and Harry Rietz, the cannery superintendent's pre-teen kids, always knew when I was coming, and would be at the parking pullout to meet me.

I worked with the kids' mother, Mary, for several winters in Haines. She taught third grade in the same building where I taught jr. high. The Rietz family spent their summers at XIP, and Libby and Harry had either radar or extra sensory perception when it came to greeting me upon arrival. They were two of the nicest kids I've ever been around, and I really enjoyed seeing them each time I flew in to XIP.

I was assigned an XIP pickup one blustery overcast afternoon. We had flown a survey crew of three men and their gear into XIP earlier. They were surveying a remote subdivision that was going to be offered for sale in a State of Alaska land auction. The crew had been there for a couple of weeks, remote even from the cannery, as they were working several miles away at the head of the inlet.

They finished their surveying job, and now they were back at the cannery and eager to return to Juneau. They called our office, and said, "We're ready. Come and get us," so Midge sent me to get them.

The only thing they "forgot" to mention is that a fourth member of their crew had flown in later with another air taxi, so now I had four passengers instead of three, and the fourth fellow had brought not only his personal gear and surveying tools, he'd also brought a pretty good sized "boom box", a supposedly portable radio, tape deck, and CD player.

Good grief, where was I going to put all this stuff, and could I get off the ground without going into the trees on the other end of the runway?

They were really anxious to get back to the bright lights of town after two weeks of isolation at the head of Excursion Inlet, so when I told them some of their stuff, or one of the guys, was going to have to stay behind, they weren't too happy. One of them started ragging me with a "If you were a *real* pilot ..." routine, so I said "Tell you what, I'm a real enough pilot that I'll leave you *all* here. I can be out of here inside of a minute, and I'm on the verge of doing just that."

"Oh! Oh! Wait a minute. Let's not be hasty. What do you want us to leave behind?"

I thought they might see it my way.

We stacked three heavy boxes of canned food, a camp stove, and two big tool boxes in the little 3-sided shelter near the end of the runway, all covered with a big heavy canvas tarp so old and full of holes that I didn't understand why they wanted it any way. The one fellow wouldn't leave his boom box, so he carried it on his lap, with his sleeping bag stacked on top of it.

I taxied as far back up the street as I could possibly get, stood on the brakes and opened the throttle until we were at full power, and then started down the runway. About three fourths of the way down the runway I dropped a notch of flaps for the extra lift, and we came off the ground. I still wasn't sure we were going to make it, but as we got up a few feet we picked up the headwind that the trees had been blocking, and cleared the trees by twenty feet or so.

Glancing back, I saw that the three back-seaters were staring down at the trees with *very* serious looks on their faces.

The head surveyor leaned over and said "Man, I'm sure glad we left that other stuff behind."

I just looked at him and grinned an "I told you so!" grin at him.

The next day one of our other pilots delivered some freight to XIP and brought the surveyor's overload back to Juneau with him. Haines Airways didn't charge them. It was just part of the service.

I first saw the guy when Joann, our Juneau ticket agent, called me out of our back freight room/pilot's lounge. "There's a gentleman out front that would like to talk to one of the pilots about Excursion Inlet."

I was the only pilot there, so I guessed that meant me, and walked out to the front counter.

The man was about 50 years old, a good-looking fellow with wavy salt-and-pepper hair that had obviously been styled. He introduced himself and offered his hand, exuding an aura of charm, self-confidence, and wealth.

"My wife and I have flown up from Illinois, and we're interested in buying some property in Excursion Inlet. We're going to fly over there today, and I've heard that the runway there is a little tricky. Can you tell me anything about it?"

"Sure can," I said. "In fact, I'm headed over that way in half an hour or so myself. What are you flying?"

"A Beechcraft Bonanza," he said.

"That makes it pretty simple then," I replied. "Don't go!"

He looked at me with a mixture of indignation and condescension, and said, "You don't understand. I can fly that Bonanza anywhere. I'm IFR rated, and have nearly a thousand hours total time."

"Well," I said, "you can do anything you want, of course, but it's very windy today, with heavy gusts, and Excursion Inlet is a real blow hole. The runway over there is very short and narrow and it has a dogleg. There are some obstructions that make the approach pretty tricky. I've been in there dozens of times, and I'm not sure I'll get in there today. I do have a pickup over there, but if it's blowing too bad, I won't even try to land."

Just then a slender attractive blonde woman in her early thir-ties came walking up and put her arm through his. He greeted her with "Hello dear. This man says it might be a little turbulent going in to Excursion Inlet today." (*Hey man, that's not what I said. I said "Don't go!"*)

"Well, I'm not afraid of a few little bumps, are you?" she grinned.

"Absolutely not," he said, "Let's grab a bite to eat and then we'll fly out there."

The south wind just howls up Chatham Strait sometimes. It comes in from the open Pacific, and Chatham funnels it up through the northern part of Southeast Alaska.

The west wind screams in from the open Pacific, and is funneled into the inland waters by Icy Strait.

Warm moist air rises from the inland waterways, and cold air funnels down off the Glacier Bay and Juneau Icefields. All of these factors come together on occasion, and Excursion Inlet sits right in the middle of that area of confluence. Sometimes the turbulence is unbelievable.

I departed Juneau for XIP in a Cherokee Six, and heard the tower clear a Bonanza for takeoff just as I departed the Juneau con-trol zone. The Bonanza was five minutes behind me, but is a faster aircraft, so I figured he'd catch me.

Sure enough, not long after I rounded Point Couverden I spot-ted a V-tailed Bonanza quite a ways off to my right and a little lower, passing me. We were both headed for XIP.

The turbulence was already bad enough that I had slowed down, but the Bonanza apparently was at cruise power, because he passed me pretty quickly.

We were within 4 or 5 miles of Excursion, and the Bonanza was a couple of miles ahead of me, when over the radio came a woman's terrified scream. I looked ahead, located the Bonanza, and saw that its wings were almost vertical, and it was still rolling. Apparently the pilot had inadvertently pressed the mike button on his control wheel when the turbulence started to roll him, so his wife's screams were being broadcast to the world. The Bonanza rolled farther and farther. He wasn't clear over on his back, but must have rolled 140 degrees at least. His wife continued screaming and sobbing as he fought the roll and finally managed to come back onto an even keel and take his thumb off the mike button.

Even from that distance I could see the Bonanza wobbling and bouncing all over the sky as he tried to keep it under control, get it turned around, and out of the severe beating they were taking. I was afraid the aircraft couldn't take it, and would fail structurally, but he finally got it turned around and headed back out of the severe turbulence.

I didn't even think about going any farther. After seeing that fiasco I wasn't about to attempt XIP. I turned around and started back to Juneau.

The Bonanza beat me back, of course, and when the couple walked past our counter Joann hailed them and asked them how their flight went.

The man replied curtly, "We decided not to buy property out there after all."

Joann said the woman didn't say anything, but she looked really *pale.*

# Chapter Nineteen
## MEDEVACS AND TRANSPORTS

Small Alaskan towns like Haines have only limited medical facilities. Sometimes there is a clinic with several doctors available, sometimes the local clinic has only a physician's assistant or a nurse practitioner, and sometimes there is only a village health aide or an EMT or two. Serious injury or illness requires transport to either Juneau or Sitka, since in northern Southeast Alaska only those two cities have real hospitals.

Bartlett Memorial Hospital in Juneau is the destination of choice for most medevacs, although occasionally a patient will be sent to the SEARHC/Mt. Edgecumbe Hospital in Sitka.

Air taxis will put themselves to no end of trouble to make sure a patient gets to expert medical care as quickly and smoothly as possible.

I was an EMT-II, and captain of the Haines Volunteer Ambulance Service for several years, so I saw medevacs from both sides of the picture. If no doctor or nurse could be spared to accompany a patient, one of our ambulance crew volunteers would go with them. No medevac patient was ever flown out without some kind of medical personnel with them.

Most of our medevacs were either trauma patients, heart patients or internal problems, although we were involved with a couple of childbirths. Patients would be stabilized and "packaged" at the local clinic, and then transported by ambulance to the airport where a Six would be waiting, with one middle and one backseat removed. A stretcher fit perfectly into the seatless open area, so the attendant could sit in either the middle or back remaining seat, and have full access to the patient. Whether we went to Juneau or Sitka, the medevac plane would be cleared to land immediately, and an ambulance with medical personnel aboard would be waiting to transport our patient directly to the hospital.

Many of our medevac patients would ride back home with us several days (or weeks) after their medevac, but occasionally the person would be gone forever. I never lost a patient while airborne, either as an EMT or as a pilot, but I do remember one elderly heart patient that expired just as we got her stretcher loaded into the aircraft. We performed CPR in the airplane for 20 minutes, but were unsuccessful in the end.

One young mother added to our passenger manifest while airborne. She was in premature labor, and was presenting breech on top of it, so she and a doctor were loaded into an airplane and headed for Juneau. Only the mother-to-be and doctor were in the back to start with, but shortly after the aircraft departed a baby girl arrived, so the passenger list grew from three to four. The baby and mother were kept in Bartlett Hospital for awhile because the baby was a preemie, but infant, mother and pilot all survived and did well.

Medevacs were never treated lightly, because the pilot knew that the patient's condition was serious, often a matter of life or death. Otherwise there wouldn't be a medevac in the first place. They were very satisfying to fly, though, because a unique bond almost always formed between the patient and the pilot due to their shared experience.

Alaska historically has had a young population, so many medevacs ended happily, with the patient returning restored to good health. As the population's average age has risen, a higher percentage of medevacs end in the patient's demise, so occasionally one of my transports would be a body returning home for burial. These flights are very sober affairs, to be sure, as I would often be bringing a friend, neighbor, or acquaintance on his or her last trip home, and then for the next several days would also be flying relatives and friends to and from the funeral.

A more odious type of transport would occur when someone was either accused or convicted of a major crime, and would have to be transported to Juneau in police custody. If the person was local, it was very likely that I at least knew who they were. I might even be acquainted with them, or may have had them as a student in school a few years previously.

During my air taxi years I transported thieves, embezzlers, arsonists, child molesters and murderers, among others. In every case the person in custody was handcuffed, our one-and-only state trooper sat right beside him/her, and another police officer, usually a city policeman, sat right in front. When we landed in Juneau we all sat in the airplane until two more Alaska State Troopers came out to the plane. One of them would open the door, and then the prisoner would be unloaded and all four would escort him to a vehicle and haul him off to jail.

It was pretty serious business, because I knew I wouldn't be seeing that person again for a long time, if ever.

Mentally ill people occasionally had to be transported too. They were usually handled in the same way criminal transports were, except often they were in straitjackets instead of handcuffs.

Cheryl, one of the dispatchers in Haines, called me in one day and told me I had a flight to transport a mental patient to Juneau. Usually we tried to do all these criminal and mental transports in a six-place airplane so the transportee could be seated in the back row, as far from the pilot as possible.

Today all of our sixes were busy, so Cheryl said I'd have to take 808, a four-place Cessna 182.

I drove out to the airport, and shortly a police car arrived with four officers and the patient, a very tall skinny young man in his mid-20s. He was a newcomer to town, but I'd seen him around a few times, always talking to himself and picking "things" off his arms and chest, so I wasn't too surprised to see him in custody. I was surprised to see him handcuffed with his hands in front, rather than in a straitjacket.

I had the police seat the patient in the right rear, with the state trooper sitting next to him (*behind me*) and the city policeman sitting in the right front (*in front of the patient*). All the seat belts were fastened, I started the engine, and taxied out. Everything seemed under control, but I was a little leery of the patient sitting so close to me. He was about 6'6," and had lo-o-ng arms, but I figured if he started acting up I'd just do some violent maneuvering to keep him off-balance until the two policemen could get things under control again.

It was a pretty day, so at least three of us were looking out and enjoying the scenery.

About half way to Juneau I caught some motion out of the corner of my eye. The patient had leaned forward and reached both hands out toward Jerry, the policeman in front of him. Bill, the state trooper, was on him in a flash, grabbing his hands and forcing them back down onto his lap, shaking his head "no" at the same time. The patient subsided ... for a minute or two.

He did it again - leaned forward and reached toward the back of Jerry's neck. Bill grabbed him again, and the patient quieted right down.

By now I'm paying more attention to the back seat than I am to where we're going.

Every two or three minutes the patient would bend forward and make reaching motions with his hands, but I noticed that he wasn't actually trying to grab Jerry, he was just shoving his handcuffed hands out in front of him, and in Jerry's direction.

Bill noticed too, and apparently figured the patient was just seeing pink elephants or something, and got into the rhythm of the thing. The patient would slowly bend and reach, and Bill would just reach up and slowly and gently put the young man's hands back down on his lap, all the while shaking his head and saying "No!", as you might to a two year old.

We entered the Juneau control zone and were cleared to land. Halfway between Coghlan Island and The Cut, on a long straight-in final approach, the kid bent forward again, but this time he moved like lightning. He lunged ahead as far as he could, reached all the way up to the back of Jerry's head ... and gently ran his fingertips all the way down Jerry's neck from his ears to his shoulders ... while giggling maniacally at the top of his voice! "Heeheeheehee."

Bill grabbed him and slammed his hands down, but meanwhile I thought Jerry was going to go right through the front windshield. He was plastered against the instrument panel as tight as he could be with his seatbelt still fastened. If there had been dual controls in 808 Jerry would have put us straight down into Auke Bay.

Bill forcibly held the kid's hands down all through the rest of the landing, and Jerry finally peeled himself off the instrument panel just as we stopped and I shut the engine down.

Jerry was still breathing hard and the kid was still giggling hysterically when the four officers got him out of the airplane and took him away.

Harold Light was tending his subsistence net in the Chilkat River, upstream from the village of Klukwan, twenty miles north of Haines. His net had one end anchored out in the river, and the other end attached to the shore. When salmon swam upstream to spawn, they would get entangled in the net, and their splashes would attract his attention. The young man could then move his small canoe hand-over-hand along the net until he could reach down and grab the fish and put it in the canoe.

Something went dreadfully wrong, though. The canoe capsized and Harold, dressed in a heavy jacket and hip boots, was thrown into the river. Others on the shore saw him fall in, but he went under and was never seen again. Searchers went up and down the river the rest of the day, but the young man was gone.

His parents were devastated, but the fact that his body hadn't been recovered was especially hard to take.

For three days in a row I loaded several family members into a Haines Airways airplane, sometimes a Cherokee Six, other times a Cessna 182, and we carefully flew each bank of the river at minimum altitude, over and over again, searching for any trace of the young man. Apparently his boots and pockets filled with river sand and glacial silt that weighed him down and prevented his body from surfacing. He was never found.

Those were such sad, sad flights.

# Chapter Twenty
## CHARTERS

I really like charters. The pilot gets to go somewhere out of the ordinary, and often there's no set itinerary, especially with people who just want to see Glacier Bay or fly around over the local area.

One family, consisting of the two parents, one teenager, and two pre-teens, showed up in the office early one morning and wanted to charter to Sitka. The couple had lived in Sitka for a short time right after they were married, but their children had never been there. They just wanted to go over for the day, but couldn't schedule that on the Alaska Airlines jet or on the state ferry.

I had also lived in Sitka back in the '60s, so Midge asked me "Hey, Cap'n Bob. How would you like to go to Sitka for the whole day?"

"Maybe," I said. "What's the scoop?"

"This family of five wants to charter to Sitka, spend the day, and then come back. They're willing to pay charter rate for the round trip, plus all the airplane's ground time over there."

"Well, that's fine for the company, but I'm only going to get paid for the round trip flight time, and then I'll miss any other flights back here. I don't think so."

"Wait a minute while I go talk to the boss" she said. By the time this particular charter took place Ernie and Reggie had sold Haines Airways to Mike Shallcross. Mike's wife Barbara was a pilot, as was his stepson, Ken Tyler. Mike's other stepson, Phil Tyler, was acting as business manager. Mike's daughter Melanie was keeping the books. Mike and Melanie were from Atlanta, "Jawjah," but Barbara, Ken, and Phil were from New Zealand. They told me that if I kept practicing I could probably eventually learn to speak "propah" English. I grinned and I told them I didn't think there was any hope for them at all.

Midge came back in just a minute and said "Mike says you're right, so we'll pay you half flight pay for all the time you're on the ground in Sitka today."

Half an hour later we were in the air headed for Sitka. The couple wanted to see some of the places they had visited by boat when they lived there, so we stayed fairly low (*1,000 feet*) even though it was a beautiful sunny day. We followed the beaches through Peril Strait and flew over Nakwasina Sound and Katlian Bay into Sitka Sound. They wanted to get a close look at Mt. Edgecumbe, the dormant volcano that is Sitka's famous landmark, so we flew out there and circled the cone. We were on the ground in Sitka by 9:30, and arranged to meet back at the airplane at 7 p.m.

I spent an hour prowling around downtown Sitka, and then visited old friends. I had lunch with one family, went halibut fishing for a few hours with another, and had an early supper with a third.

We took off from Sitka for Haines at 7:30 and enjoyed a beautifully smooth evening flight directly back to Haines. This air taxi job is really rough sometimes, but someone has to do it.

The charter flight into Snettisham, 35 miles southeast of Juneau, to deliver fish food to the salmon hatchery is spectacular. The flight path traverses some of the most ruggedly scenic non-glacial country in Southeast. There are steep, rugged mountains and long, deep, narrow ocean inlets. I don't remember ever flying in there without seeing brown bears somewhere along the way. The flight into Snettisham is marvelous.

Snettisham itself is the pits.

The airstrip is at the head of a long, narrow inlet, and it rises steadily from the beach to its upper end. Steep rugged mountains closely surround it, so you can only land in one direction (*uphill*), and you can only take off in one direction (*downhill*).

Once you land, one of the hatchery personnel might drive a truck down to the strip, but they don't always hear a landing airplane. In any case, an air taxi pilot always has to load and unload his own airplane, so 30 bags of fish food might go onto a truck, or they might end up neatly stacked at the upper end of the runway.

In the meantime, Snettisham in the summer is the buggiest place in the world. There are mosquitoes the size of hummingbirds, and black flies thicker than a plague of locusts. Once the plane is on the ground and the door opened, your only thought is "how quickly can I get this done and get out of here."

The flight back to Juneau is superb.

Dry Bay, near the northern end of Glacier Bay National Monument, is another enjoyable charter destination, provided the weather is halfway decent.

In 1943 or '44 the military bulldozed an airstrip a few miles south of Yakutat beside the Alsek River. It was long enough to handle DC-3s. Since then rafting trips down the Alsek-Tatshenshini River System have become extremely popular. These rafting parties assemble in Haines, are taken by truck up into the Yukon Territory to the headwaters of the Alsek or the Tat, and 10 days later they arrive at the Dry Bay airstrip. These trips are so much in demand that the U.S. Park Service regulates the number of rafters that can use the river during any one summer, in order to preserve the wild aspects of the river system.

Haines Airways was regularly called to come and get float parties and ferry them and their gear back to Haines. As many as three airplanes would be dispatched to Dry Bay, and if the weather was good and we could go direct, we would fly right over the top of Glacier Bay, in the shadow of Mt. Fairweather *(15,300 ft.)*, the tallest mountain in Southeast Alaska, and then down the Grand Pacific and Alsek Glaciers and across Alsek Lake and into Dry Bay airstrip.

A direct flight meant that we had to climb to 8,000 feet to clear the mountains, so we could see for miles and miles. In good weather the flight was fantastically beautiful, and ... *and, for dessert!* ... at Dry Bay we could get strawberries. The flats surrounding the airstrip were covered with wild strawberry plants. The berries were always small, and never really turned red, but, oh, were they sweet and good.

Alsek Glacier and Alsek Lake, near Dry Bay. Glacier Bay National Park – Summer, 1993

The strawberries got me in trouble on one occasion. The Dry Bay airstrip is sandy, and the turn-arounds at both ends are quite soft. That's usually no problem. As long as the pilot keeps his taxi speed up, he can wheel right through the soft spots and get back onto the firmer parts of the strip.

On this particular day one of the rafters had wandered down past the end of the runway in search of strawberries. When I landed, he ran out onto the turnaround, intending to flag me down and beg a ride back to the mid-field parking area. His intention was to be available to help load the airplane and not slow things down.

Instead, he forced me to stop, and the aircraft was stuck in the soft sand. Instead of a ride back to the parking area, he had to hike down there, get the rest of his party, and hike back so they could all push me through the sand and onto the firmer runway.

On another trip to Dry Bay I ran into clouds near the top of the Tsirku Glacier, and had to "shoot the gap" in order to get through. Two hours later I was returning, this time with one passenger and a full load of rafts and equipment. By then the cloud layer had settled right down onto the top of the glacier, even though most of the countryside was bathed in bright sunshine.

Since the Tsirku is only about five miles long, and I knew from previous experience that the glacier's edge was as straight as a string and came out a thousand feet above the floor of Tahkeen Valley, I flew over to the south edge, a few hundred feet above the glacier's surface, and descended through the cloud, keeping visual reference to the edge where the blue glacial ice met the green mountainside.

Two or three minutes later we emerged from the cloud, and into the bright sunshine in the valley. Only then did I realize that my passenger was staring out the front window, and was holding his breath. When he finally was able to breathe again, he asked "How did you know where we were when I couldn't see my hand in front of my face?"

"Sorry I worried you," I replied. "I was watching the mountain out the side window. I knew exactly where we were all the time."

Two middle-aged couples came into the office one morning and wanted to charter an airplane "to see the local area." They looked at our big aeronautical chart displayed on the waiting area's wall, conferred among themselves for awhile, and decided that they would like to see Glacier Bay.

Cheryl offered them our standard one-hour GBT, but they declined, saying they wanted to see things off of the beaten track. Charter rates were discussed and agreed on, and I was summoned out of the back room.

"These folks want to see the local area," she told me, "and they've chartered 75 Whiskey. You'll be their pilot."

We got acquainted a bit on the ride out to the airport, and when we departed I thought I had a pretty good idea of what they wanted to see. I took them straight over the top to Johns Hopkins Inlet, with its spectacular glaciers and hundreds of floating icebergs. They were definitely impressed, but decided they wanted to see Mt. Fairweather while they in the vicinity, so we circled clear out to the Pacific coast so they could see the mountain from all sides.

On the way back to Haines they decided they wanted to see how the Juneau Icecap compared with Glacier Bay, so we went straight east and up on top of the Icecap, wandering back and forth to "see all the sights."

One of the men asked to see an aeronautical chart of the area, and he soon realized that the Icecap went all the way to Juneau and beyond. "Why don't we fly all the way down the Icecap to Juneau?" asked one of the ladies. So we did.

I kept in radio contact with the Haines office as much as possible, so they knew when we deviated from the original plan in Glacier Bay, knew we had crossed Lynn Canal and gone up on the Icecap, and knew we were meandering south towards Juneau.

When we got to the Mendenhall I told the folks we were going to have to land in Juneau for fuel. That was fine with them. They bought me lunch at the Juneau airport restaurant, and purchased some souvenirs at the gift shop.

Then they let me in on the "new" plan. The ladies wanted to go to Sitka, and the men wanted to see what Hoonah was like, so I filed a Hoonah-Sitka-Haines flight plan with Juneau Radio, telephoned the Haines office one last time, and set off for Hoonah.

Twenty minutes later we were on the ground, where the two couples hired a taxi to take them on a half-hour tour of downtown Hoonah, while I waited with the airplane.

As soon as they returned we loaded up and headed for Sitka, 45 minutes farther south. We detoured out to Kruzof Island so they could get a close look at Mt. Edgecumbe, and then landed at the Sitka airport.

Another taxi took us all into town, where we proceeded to go from shop to shop until it was time for supper. After we ate, another taxi took us back to the plane, and we flew directly from Sitka back to Haines. I had a great time, got two free meals out of the deal, and the company and I were both paid for 6.1 hours of flight time plus 3.5 hours of standby.

Three of us were sent to Dry Bay one summer day to get a party of eight rafters, with two rafts, and all their personal gear. One Cherokee was the "passenger" plane. He would take five passengers and all the personal gear he had room for. The second was the "mixed cargo and pax" plane. He took his back two seats out, so he'd have the other three passengers, plus room for some of their bulky stuff. I was the "straight cargo" aircraft. I took out my back two rows of seats so I could take the heavy bulky things, mainly the rafts and the raft frames, tents, and things like that.

Will it all fit? It already did! This pile of baggage, plus three adult passengers, just came from Dry Bay, haul-out point for Alsek-Tatshenshini rafting trips. Cherokee Sixes are excellent cargo haulers, and have often been described as "flying pickup trucks." Haines Airport – July, 1995

We all arrived and found the rafters all pretty much packed up and ready to go. Most of their gear was packed in dry bags, the rafts were both rolled up and tied, and one of the raft frames was broken down and in pieces, ready to be loaded aboard. The other frame, a solid model, was leaning against a small tree. I'm sure it was no problem to load that frame onto the two-ton truck that took this party from Haines up to the headwaters of the Alsek, but it was not going to go into a Cherokee Six.

We had been confronted with this kind of situation a few times before, so it was now SOP (*standard operating procedure*) that whenever we had a flight out of Dry Bay, one of the planes carried a hacksaw and some extra blades. I went back to my airplane, got the hacksaw, and went over to the solid frame and started to cut it in pieces.

The poor raft owner hadn't been paying too much attention until he saw me start in on his frame with the saw. Then he just about went into orbit.

"WHAT ARE YOU DOING?" he shouted. "Don't you know those frames cost over $2,000?"

"Well, as a matter of fact I *do* know they cost that much," I replied while I continued to saw. "That's why I figured you'd want to take it with you rather than leave it here under this tree."

"What do you mean?" he huffed.

I quit sawing, straightened up, and said, "As you can see, your raft frame is *not* going to fit into this airplane the way it is now, so as I see it you have three choices. You can charter a DC-3 to come in here and get it, or you can just leave it here, OR we can cut it up into manageable pieces and when you get it back home it will cost you a hundred bucks to have some welding shop turn it into a break-apart frame for you. It's your choice, but I think I know what I would do if I were in your shoes."

He looked at his frame, looked over at the Cherokee, and then held out his hand and said, "I'll saw for awhile."

My charter destination list for just one summer (*1993*) reads like an atlas of northern Southeast Alaska. I flew a charter flight to Whitehorse, Yukon Territory, where we all had to wait in the airplane for an hour because Canadian Customs didn't show up when we landed. Either the FAA didn't forward our flight plan to

Whitehorse right away, or Whitehorse misplaced it. Neither party would 'fess up.

I flew a group of steelhead fishermen to Yakutat, and went to Dry Bay several times to pick up rafting parties. I went into Excursion Inlet six or seven times, and picked up several hundred pounds of frozen salmon in Hoonah that were on their way to Japan, via Juneau and Anchorage.

A mill owner and his wife chartered to Petersburg with a layover of four hours. I went to Kake, where we had to buzz a black bear off the runway before we could land, and to Sitka a couple of times, one of them a medevac.

This list doesn't begin to take into account the GBT and Icecap charters, or the aerial photographers who wanted to shoot glaciers, not caring which one, or the folks who just wanted to fly around a little and see what the area looked like from the air.

Every day brought something different and enjoyable.

# Chapter Twenty One
## OOPS!

Every endeavor that involves human beings has an occasional "Oops!" occurrence. Sometimes the incident is just amusing, sometimes it's terrifically funny. Sometimes it's a near miss, sometimes there is minor damage to property or dignity, and occasionally it's serious or even tragic, but there's *always* a lesson from the "School of Hard Knocks" or one of its adjunct campuses.

During my twelve summers of air taxi flights I had very few hints of mechanical trouble. I had an injector plug up right after takeoff once, and had to go around the pattern and land with only five cylinders producing power while the sixth cylinder produced only very noticeable hiccups. On two other occasions I experienced a momentary loss of power when the engine swallowed a bit of water. That gets your heart rate up in a hurry, but both times the engine immediately picked up again.

The closest I ever came to having an accident due to mechanical failure occurred when I had a tire blow out just as I touched down on the Dry Bay gravel airstrip. The aircraft, traveling about eighty miles per hour, slewed violently to the left and headed for the trees. I trimmed a fair number of finger-sized alders before I managed to get straightened out again and back on the runway, but I didn't dare stop then, because I knew if I stopped I'd never get an airplane with a flat tire taxiing again on the sandy airstrip. The entire runway would be blocked unless I could taxi off the runway.

I kept the plane rolling with lots of power and lots of right rudder until I got it into the mid-field parking area, and then shut it down. It looked pretty forlorn sitting there with its left wingtip almost dragging in the dirt.

The park ranger there had an emergency radiophone, so I asked him to contact our office in Haines and explain the situation.

Ninety minutes later one of our mechanics came winging into Dry Bay in his own plane. We recruited a group of rafters to get under the left wing and hold it up high enough and long enough to change tires. Shortly after that we were loaded and on our way back to Haines.

❖

For the past couple of weeks Ken Tyler had been talking about a scheme he and Tom, the owner of the Fairweather Country Inn in Gustavus, had dreamed up. Instead of flying Tom's clients to the Gustavus Airport and having Tom pick them up in a van, we (*Haines Airways*) would fly them from Juneau directly to his lodge. We would land in the meadow behind the lodge and drop our passengers right at the lodge's door. When they were ready to leave, we'd fly in, pick them up, and fly them directly back to Juneau.

Is the meadow big enough to land and takeoff with a fully loaded Cherokee Six?

"I'm pretty sure it is," said Tom to Ken. "I fly my Cessna 170 in and out of there all the time."

Ken kept mentioning this plan, talking about how lucrative it would be for the company, and what a neat experience it would be for the lodge clients. Circumstances seemed to conspire against him though, and for the next couple of weeks he never ended up in Gustavus with enough extra time to check out Fairweather Country Inn's grass strip.

Joann, our Juneau station agent, came into the back room one afternoon about 3:30 and told me my next flight would be a 5 p.m. pickup in Gustavus, with the passengers to be taken to Haines.

Gustavus is only a 20 minute flight from Juneau, so I thought to myself "If I go over there right now, I'll have time to check out the grass strip, and then jump the five miles to Gustavus airport for my pickup. Ho ho - something new and exciting!"

Forty-five minutes later I was circling Tom's meadow at 500 feet. I flew across it a couple of times, timing the crossing so I could estimate how long the meadow was. I flew a 170 of my own, and I knew it would get in and out of fields a *lot* shorter than a fully loaded Cherokee Six could manage.

I calculated that the meadow was long enough to land a Cherokee, so I circled out a mile or so away from my touchdown point, and set up a power-on short-field landing. I touched down right on the end of the meadow, ducked around one lone tree growing out in the center of the area, and applied moderate braking.

The first thing I noticed was that the "meadow" was covered with grass nearly 2 feet high. I could hear it swishing vigorously against the landing gear and underside of the fuselage and wings, and could see seed heads and stalks flying all over as the prop cut a swath through the grass.

I got the airplane slowed down enough to do a 180 degree turn, stopped, turned off the engine and got out of the airplane. No one had come out of the lodge yet, in spite of my low circles around the area, so I started walking toward the lodge.

I got perhaps 50 feet past the rear of the airplane when I came to a lovely little ditch about 18 inches deep, neatly hidden in the tall grass. Oops! Another 50 feet on my rollout and I would have hit that ditch. That would have ruined a perfectly good day... and a perfectly good airplane, or at least the prop and nose gear.

Nobody ever came out of the lodge, in spite of all my low level shenanigans. Tom must not have been home, so I went back to the airplane and took off, flew the few miles to Gustavus airport, landed, and picked up my passengers and flew them to Haines.

The airplane, painted white with green and gold trim, had great green stains all over the landing gear, belly, and wings. The grass seed blown all over inside the engine compartment made it smell like burning popcorn for the next week.

Ken flew the plane the next day, and afterward asked me, "Where in the *world* did you take that airplane?"

"Ken," I replied, "don't even *think* about delivering passengers to the Fairweather Country Inn."

"Oh."

That's the last we heard about that particular idea, and I learned another "Oops" lesson.

"Hey, you guys should be interested in this," the Skagway Air ticket agent said as she hung up the phone. "There's a squadron of Lake Amphibian "touristas" due in here any minute."

Several of us were sitting in the Skagway airport terminal, waiting for buses to deliver our GBT passengers. The phone call had come from the SkagAir agent in Juneau, who thought the mass arrival of fifteen Lake Amphibians in Skagway would be of sufficient interest to arouse a host of spectators.

Sure enough, the word spread, and 10 minutes later there were thirty or forty people standing outside the terminal building, scanning the southern sky for the first sign of the Lakes' arrival.

Shortly we spotted the gaggle of Lakes, flying in a big loose flock. Apparently they had some kind of pecking order established, because they started to string out, with some coming straight in to land on Runway One, and others circling to wait their turn. They certainly weren't as efficient at landing as the local air taxi fleet, but on the other hand, they couldn't be expected to be, either. They were essentially "strangers in paradise," landing on a strange airport, and not familiar with the local customs or layouts. "Better safe than sorry" is a very sound piece of advice.

The parking lot was already fairly full, so these folks were probably going to need some help. A couple of the SkagAir pilots went out on the apron to direct traffic, showing the transients to parking spots and guiding them in.

One of the later arrivals was directed to a spot between two of his recently arrived friends, and as he pulled forward into the parking place, the SkagAir director saw that the slot wasn't wide enough and signaled the Lake pilot to stop where he was, slightly behind his buddies.

Apparently the Laker thought he knew better, because he gunned his engine, slid up between his friends, and clipped both wingtips, tearing out one wingtip light on his right, another on his left, and ripping out both of his own marker lights ... in front of forty spectators.

Oops! Another six inches and it would have been OK.

Right after Aleta and I moved to Haines my neighbor Ken Rischer acquired a pretty little Luscombe, an all-metal two-place taildragger produced in the early 1950s. Ken was in his late forties, and really wanted to learn to fly. He read everything he could about flying, and his conversations all involved flying in one way or another. He wanted to fly so badly that he bought the Luscombe so he would have an airplane to learn in.

As soon as his Luscombe was delivered he scheduled his first lesson with the only certified flight instructor in town. For one reason or another, his first lesson was also his last lesson. The CFI swore to never again set foot in any kind of airplane with him, and he, in turn, described the CFI in less-than-loving four-letter terms.

The situation didn't look too good for the aspiring pilot. He had an airplane, but no instructor, so he did what *he* thought was the only logical thing he could do ... he taught himself to fly.

He started by taxiing slowly up and down the taxiway for an hour or so. Then he started taxiing a little faster, and then faster yet. After several evenings of taxi practice he went out on the runway and practiced taxiing fast enough to get the tail off the ground.

From there on it was a short step to a full-throttle taxi, and then a bit of back pressure and the plane was airborne. The Luscombe is a fairly sprightly aircraft, but Ken managed to fly the Luscombe around for awhile, getting the feel of it, and eventually had to figure out how to land again. He ended up driving it onto the runway in a full-throttle wheel landing. After the wheels touched he cut the throttle and let the plane roll out until the tail dropped and he could apply brakes and stop. His landing took most of the 3,000 foot runway.

I know ... I know ..., but every word is true. That's exactly what he did, and continued to do. I don't know how many hours he amassed. He wasn't keeping track, but he flew often. All of his flights were at full throttle, and all of his landings were the same - full throttle and wheel it on. He flew low, and he flew fast, and he was a disaster waiting to happen.

Ken knew that I had my pilot's license, and he also knew that I hadn't been able to fly for several years. He asked me to go flying with him numerous times, but I always had some excuse. Finally I just had to tell him, "Ken, I'm sorry, but I wouldn't set foot in an airplane with you as pilot for anything in the world."

He just laughed and continued his self-instructed flying "lessons."

One spring day a few months later I drove out to the airport to visit my friend Ernie.

As I drove up and parked I noticed my neighbor Ken examining the prop spinner of his Luscombe and looking very serious. He turned and watched me as I walked over to say hello, but he didn't say anything. He just kept looking at the nose of his airplane. As I got to him I also glanced at the front of his plane.

Dead center across his bright red prop spinner was a deep dent with several long scratches on each side. I turned and looked questioningly at him, and he glanced down at the left wheel pant, much like a fender for streamlining a wheel, and nodded. More deep scratches marred its surface. As I turned to him again he glanced up at the right wing. Still more deep scratches snaked across the empty spot on the leading edge where the landing light lens used to be. I could hardly believe what I was seeing.

"What in the world did you *do?*" I asked. I was astounded!

"You know that cable car crossing up at 26 Mile on the Chilkat River? Well, Keith *(Whiting, another local pilot, and owner of an Alon Aircoupe)* and I were dogfighting up the valley and I got on his tail. He went low-level down on the river and tried to shake me by flying under the cable car. I didn't see it in time, and flew through the steel cable."

Oops! and double oops! A frightening lesson from the School of Severe Chastening.

*The scratches and dents showed that Ken had hit that steel cable in the exact center of his prop spinner. If he had been as much as an inch off in any direction, the cable collision would have definitely caused him to crash right there on the river. As it was, one end of the severed cable had whipped down across the wheel pant, the other had whipped up across the leading edge of the wing, and Ken flew away with only minor damage to his airplane and his ego.*

A few weeks later Ken was a passenger in a chartered Cherokee air taxi that crashed and burned in bad weather near Petersburg. All six people aboard were killed on impact. The NTSB Accident Report (5) stated:

Part 135 Nonscheduled operation of XXX FLYING SER
Aircraft: PIPER PA-34, registration: NXXXXX
PETERSBURG, AK

PILOT DATA: AGE 24, 1683 TOTAL HOURS, COMMER-CIAL, CFI, 1 0 0 COMMERCIAL, 45 IN TYPE

DEPARTURE POINT: HAINES, AK

INTENDED DESTINATION: WRANGELL, AK

TYPE OF ACCIDENT : COLLISION WITH GROUND/WATER

PHASE OF OPERATION: IN FLIGHT - UNCON-TROLLED DESCENT

PROBABLE CAUSE(S): MISCELLANEOUS - UNDETER-MINED

FACTOR(S): PILOT IN COMMAND - LACK OF FA-
MILIARITY WITH AIRCRAFT PILOT IN COMMAND
– CONTINUED VFR FLIGHT INTO ADVERSE
WEATHER CONDITIONS WEATHER - LOW CEILING

WEATHER BRIEFING - BRIEFED BY FLIGHT SER-
VICE PERSONNEL, BY RADIO WEATHER FORECAST -
WEATHER SLIGHTLY WORSE THAN FORECAST

SKY CONDITION: OBSCURED CEILING AT ACCI-
DENT SITE: UNKNOWN/NOT REPORTED

VISIBILITY AT ACCIDENT SITE : UNKNOWN/
NOT REPORTED PRECIPITATION AT ACCIDENT SITE:
UNKNOWN/NOT REPORTED

OBSTRUCTIONS TO VISION AT ACCIDENT SITE: UN-
KNOWN/NOT REPORTED
TYPE OF WEATHER CONDITIONS: IFR

TYPE OF FLIGHT PLAN: VFR FIRE AFTER IMPACT

REMARKS - LOSS OF CONTROL FOR UNDETER-
MINED REASON.

Tony had attended a reputable flight school, and had his private, commercial, and instrument ratings. He may have had a multi-engine rating, too. I'm not sure.

With perseverance and lots of money, ratings in aviation aren't too hard to come by. Judgment only comes with experience, and not always then.

Tony owned a Taylorcraft, a two-place fabric taildragger related to a Piper Cub. He flew a lot, as he wanted to build time so he could go to work for an air taxi somewhere. A pilot can get all his necessary ratings in three- to four-hundred hours, but many insurance companies require air taxis to hire pilots with 1,000 hours or more of experience, hence the need to "build time."

Tony flew across Lynn Canal and landed on the dirt strip at Katzaheen Flats one early spring day. As he back-taxied he pulled off the narrow strip to turn around and ran over a deadhead hidden in the grass along the edge of the strip. He broke six inches or so off each wooden propeller blade, a mishap that automatically grounds an airplane.

The Katzaheen Flats lie on a direct flight path between Skagway and Juneau. In addition flights between Haines and Skagway come close to, though not directly over, the flats.

A number of airplanes fly over or within sight of the flats every day, but Tony apparently couldn't attract anyone's attention. He finally decided that he would have to take things into his own hands.

He pushed his Taylorcraft out of the weeds and back onto the dirt strip, fired it up, and roared down the airstrip to take off.

The prop was no longer in balance, of course, so there was considerable vibration, and even though the engine was developing full power, the amputated prop was no longer capable of producing full thrust.

The Taylorcraft limped into the air at the end of the runway, but it was incapable of climbing out of ground effect.

An aircraft is "in ground effect" when its wing is no higher than one-half of its wingspan above the ground (or any "hard" surface, like water). An extra cushion of air develops under the wing as long as the airplane is very close to the ground. As soon as the wing is higher than half of its wingspan, ground effect no longer provides that extra lift.

Tony's T-Craft had a wingspan of 34 feet. Half of that gives us a ground effect wing altitude of 17 feet. The wing is between five and six feet above the landing gear, so Tony could only get his airplane's wheels a maximum of eleven or twelve feet above the surface.

He flew across the flats, down the beach, and several miles across Lynn Canal at this altitude, wildly vibrating all the way. When he reached the other side he flew up the beach and landed in a highway pullout just a few feet above the ocean.

The FAA was not pleased with Tony's feat of aviation derring-do. Oops!

The call came over the EMS pager early one winter morning, just as it was getting light.

"Attention all firemen and ambulance crew! Attention all firemen and ambulance crew! There has been an aircraft accident at the airport. There has been an aircraft accident at the airport."

I was at school, but I didn't have a first period class, so I responded. My junior high principal, Alan Heinrich, had agreed that if I wasn't in the classroom with students I should respond to fire and ambulance calls. He was also on the fire department and ambulance crew, and we both knew how important it was for every volunteer who was able to respond to calls. He just didn't want me to leave a classroom full of junior high students alone, and he was absolutely correct in his judgment.

The column of thick black smoke was visible from town, five miles away. If that was an airplane, someone could be in *serious* trouble.

Alan and I were some of the first volunteers on the scene. A brand new Cessna 206 had gone off the north side of the runway, crossed the taxiway, and was 50 yards out in the trees, burning brightly.

We ran over as close as we could get and could see that the pilot's door and the back cargo door were both wide open and no one was in the aircraft. We did a quick trip around the entire airplane, and there were no tracks in the snow going to or from the burning 206. That seemed strange, but we didn't have too much time to think about it.

Two fire trucks, a pumper and a tanker, both manned by other volunteers, arrived just after we completed our walk-around, and everyone pitched in to put the fire out. The airplane, of course, was a total loss.

Afterwards the entire story came out. The air taxi pilot had two passengers to take to Juneau, but he couldn't get the airplane started on this cold winter morning. He tried several times, but it was no-go. Standard procedure then is to get out and turn the prop through several rotations by hand, to turn the engine over and prime the cylinders with fuel.

The pilot debated leaving his passengers in the plane while he went through this procedure, but finally decided they should all get out of the plane.

He left the throttle at half open, so gas would get into the cylinders, but he also mistakenly left the magnetos turned on. Unbeknownst to him the engine was "hot."

He pulled the prop through one cylinder, but when he started to pull it through the second time the engine fired, caught, and immediately revved up to half throttle. The plane lurched ahead, the prop almost catching the pilot. He threw himself backward to the ground, and was nearly run over by the landing gear.

The empty aircraft launched itself across the taxiway towards the runway. It ran across the frozen pond between the taxiway and the runway, gaining speed all the while, and when it hit the gentle bank on the far side of the pond it bounced up and became airborne for a very short while.

Unable to sustain flight at half throttle, it settled back down to the ground, changed directions, and went back across the taxiway and into the trees. The astounded pilot and passengers watched as it crashed and burst into flames.

Oops!

Darold and Becky Kludt, fellow teachers, owned a very clean little Piper Cherokee 140, the same type of aircraft that I originally started flying. One Thanksgiving they flew down to Juneau, and while they were there the weather turned sour, as it often does in fall and winter. They left their airplane tied down at the Juneau Airport and came home on the ferry.

One thing led to another, work and weather never cooperated, and in February their 140 was still sitting in the transient tiedowns at Juneau. Finally, after almost three months had passed, months that were marked with constantly fluctuating periods of thaw-freeze-snow-rain-repeat, the weather on a Saturday in late February cooperated, and I flew Darold down to retrieve his airplane.

The airport maintenance people had been plowing around it for ages, so the poor thing was almost buried in snow. We finally got it dug out, and when Darold opened the cockpit door, we discovered that it needed to be dug out again. The constantly varying weather had caused frost to form inside the cabin. There were layers of ice crystals up to six inches thick all over the cabin walls, roof, instrument panel, and seats. Everything inside was covered with heavy, heavy hoar frost.

Darold looked like he was ready to cry, but he knew he had to get all that frost out before he could fly his baby home.

He told me to go ahead and fly back to Haines, and he would follow as soon as he got the interior of his airplane shoveled out. I got back in time for lunch, and Darold made it just before dark.

Oops!

❖

During the time I was flying for Haines Airways I also gave flying lessons. I took students who had no experience at all and taught them up until they got their private pilot's license. I also did Biannual Flight Reviews (*a mandated every-other-year check ride and oral review*), and checked pilots out in new aircraft. Most often this would occur when a pilot was transitioning from conventional gear to a tail dragger.

Some students were quicker intellectually than others, and some were better at actually maneuvering the aircraft, but without exception every pilot and student pilot that I worked with was a very nice person.

Never during those years of instruction did we ever have a problem ... with one exception, which I'll tell you about.

Andy was a young man in his late twenties. He had been bitten *hard* by the aviation bug, and wanted to learn to fly so bad he could taste it. When I met him he and his wife had just moved to town, and he was immersing himself in ground school courses. He soon took, and passed, his private pilot ground school exam, and was ready to get into the air.

He had the time, and he had the finances, to schedule lessons at almost any time. I was available, and we had access to an airplane. Ernie and I had sold 99 Charlie (*it almost broke my heart*) the year previously, but the fellow who bought it lived in town, and I was able to rent it for instructional purposes.

There was only one drawback. Andy was a Viet Nam vet, and had lost his right arm just below the elbow. He had a prosthesis, a pair of curved hooks that he could open and close and grip things with, but he *knew* that he could never operate a round throttle knob with his hooks.

I hated to see Andy give up his dream over a something as simple as a throttle knob. All the other controls had "push-pull" knobs. We tried out the flap handle while sitting on the ground, and found that he could easily pull flaps on, but would have to reach across and raise them again with his left hand. That problem wasn't insurmountable, so the throttle knob was all that was holding him back. He *had* to be able to push and pull the throttle knob, and he *had* to be able to do it with his right "hand."

I went down to the hardware store and bought a screwdriver with the biggest plastic handle I could find. I cut the plastic handle off, and went to work on it with a file and sandpaper, transforming the handle from a cylinder into a sharply curved hourglass shape. I drilled and tapped a hole in one end, and replaced 99 Charlie's round throttle knob with the new plastic one. It worked like a charm. Andy could push and pull the throttle with no problems. Let's go fly!

My logbook shows that Andy and I did preflights, taxiing, turns, climbs and descents, stalls and 3-point landings during our next eight or nine hours of flight time together. Andy wasn't the best student I'd ever had, but he was far from the worst, and was doing nicely until one day we had a lesson scheduled and the wind was blowing 20 mph or so out of the south.

I told Andy this would be a perfect day for him to learn wheel landing techniques.

In a 3-point taildragger landing the pilot comes in slower and slower and slower, all the while raising the nose of the airplane, until the airplane stalls and quits flying. The idea is to get the airplane to touch the runway with all three wheels at the same time (3-point), and at a slow enough speed that the airplane quits flying just as it touches the runway. This is great on a calm day, but doesn't work as well in higher winds or cross winds.

In a wheel landing, the pilot flies the taildragger right on to the runway, at slower than cruise speed, but still in cruise attitude (straight and level). The main wheels touch the runway, and the pilot closes the throttle while slowly pushing forward on the control wheel. The object is to keep the tailwheel up in the air for as long as possible. As the airplane slows, the tailwheel eventually comes down, and as soon as the pilot feels the tailwheel hit the ground, he immediately applies full backpressure on the control wheel to "pin" the tailwheel to the ground. Only then is he free to apply the brakes. This technique gives the pilot better rudder control, hence better directional stability, especially when the wind is blowing.

I demonstrated the first couple of wheel landings, with Andy just sitting in the left front seat, watching and listening while I explained what I was doing. On the third landing I had him follow through with me on the controls. He seemed comfortable with that, and showed no hesitancy when I asked him if he wanted to try one, and I would follow through with him.

Around the pattern we went, downwind, base, final, short final, and he flew it on nicely about 100 yards past the approach end of the runway. So far so good.

We veered just a tad to the left, and Andy hit the right rudder pedal ... a wee bit too much ... left rudder ... right ... I was on the rudder pedals with him, trying to smooth out his oscillations, but on the third one his feet slipped higher up on the rudder pedals. Nine Nine Charlie had toe brakes, so now every time he pushed the rudder pedal he also applied the brakes. I could help with the rudder oscillations, but I couldn't pull the toe brakes back off with Andy stepping on them.

Charlie still had her tail in the air, and the braking quickly forced it higher and higher, until ... *Whoooah!* ...Thump! She stood right up on her nose in the middle of the runway, balanced on the prop spinner and the two main wheels.

Ernie was in his shop at the time and saw everything. He came over with his pickup truck, the three of us dropped Charlie back down on her tailwheel, and Ernie towed her back to his shop to be repaired. We just finished rolling her into the hangar when a fire truck and an ambulance pulled up out front. One of the drivers rolled down his window and asked, "Where's the plane crash?"

"I dunno. Was there a plane crash?"

Oops!

*(The FAA classified this as an "incident," not an "accident." An incident is much less serious. There is no NTSB investigation, and no fault or blame is placed on anyone involved. This was the only time I ever scratched the paint on an airplane.)*

The air taxi pilot had only been in Alaska for a few weeks. He was married, and had over 1,200 hours of logged flight time. He picked up five tour ship passengers for a glacier/sightseeing flight. He and another plane had circled a moose on Murphy Flats, and then saw a brown bear and cub near Pyramid Island. He circled, low and tight, so his passengers could get a good look at the bear. As he came out of his turn he was pointed up the steep mountainside. The aircraft stalled at low level when the pilot attempted to avoid the terrain, flipped over on its back, dived into the trees, and burned.

The NTSB Accident Investigation Report (6) states:

AFTER DEPARTING ON AN AIR TOUR FLIGHT, THE PILOT CIRCLED ABOUT 700 FEET ABOVE GROUND LEVEL ALONG A SHORELINE TO OBSERVE A MOOSE.

AT THE TIME, THE PILOT WAS IN RADIO COMMU-
NICATION WITH ANOTHER AIR TOUR PILOT WHO
WAS ABOUT 1/2 MILE IN TRAIL. AFTER COMPLET-
ING THE TURN ABOVE THE MOOSE, THE PILOT
WAS OBSERVED BY THE IN-TRAIL PILOT TO BEGIN
A DESCENT. THE ACCIDENT PILOT RADIOED TO
THE IN-TRAIL PILOT THAT HE WANTED TO CIRCLE
AROUND A BEAR AND HER CUBS ON THE SHORE-
LINE. THE IN-TRAIL PILOT, AS WELL AS A GROUND
WITNESS, OBSERVED THE ACCIDENT AIRPLANE INI-
TIATE TURNS TOWARD RAPIDLY RISING TERRAIN,
THEN LEVEL THE WINGS AND CLIMB IN A NOSE-
HIGH ATTITUDE TOWARD THE RISING TERRAIN.
THE AIRPLANE IMPACTED TREES ABOUT 500 FEET
ABOVE THE SHORELINE. NO DISTRESS CALLS WERE
REPORTED. EXAMINATION OF THE WRECKAGE DID
NOT REVEAL ANY EVIDENCE OF A PREIMPACT ME-
CHANICAL MALFUNCTION. AN ON-SHORE WIND OF
ABOUT 10 KNOTS PREVAILED AT THE TIME. THE DI-
RECTOR OF FLIGHT OPERATIONS STATED THAT HE
RECOMMENDS TO HIS PILOTS TO NOT CIRCLE GAME
DURING FLIGHTSEEING FLIGHTS.

The National Transportation Safety Board determines the
probable cause(s) of this accident as follows:

THE PILOT'S FAILURE TO MAINTAIN AN AD-
EQUATE ALTITUDE ABOVE AND CLEARANCE FROM
THE SURROUNDING TERRAIN. A FACTOR RELATED
TO THE ACCIDENT WAS THE PILOT'S IMPROPER
DECISION TO CONDUCT THE MANEUVER IN SUCH
CLOSE PROXIMITY TO THE RISING TERRAIN.

# Chapter Twenty Two
## MISSIONARIES AND OTHER PEOPLE

It takes all kinds to make the world go around, I guess. I had a charter from Skagway to Juneau one afternoon. My four passengers were employees from two different cruise ships that were tied up in Juneau for the day. They had flown to Skagway for a day of sight-seeing and were now ready to return to their ship in Juneau. The two couples were waiting for me when I landed in Skagway. They were four of the most attractive people I think I've ever seen. They were in their mid- to late twenties. The two women were stunningly beautiful, and could have stepped off the pages of any number of magazines, while the two guys were rugged, muscular, and hand-some beyond words. Each couple was very obviously romantically involved, giggling, touching, hugging, and smooching.

Did I feel like The Ugly Duckling?

Yep!

I had a Cherokee Six, and one couple wanted to sit in the middle row, and the other couple in the back row. They had no luggage, so we were lightly loaded, and they could sit wherever they wanted as far as I was concerned.

The flight from Skagway to Juneau was 45 minutes long, and the couple of times I looked back re-confirmed my conclusion that each couple was romantically involved. No, they weren't *that* romantically involved, but maybe almost ... anyway, after awhile I just quit look-ing back.

We landed in Juneau and I walked them into the terminal through the air taxi gate, and went over to our counter. The two couples followed me, arms around each other, joined at the hip, and apparently getting ready to go back to their separate ships.

In the middle of the airport lobby, right in front of our counter, each couple went into a full-fledged, hang-onto-your-hat, oh-my-oh-my, passionate embrace and soul kiss, lasting at least 20 seconds. Christie, our ticket agent, stopped talking to me in mid-sentence and stared open-mouthed, it was that good!

As the embraces ended, each person slowly stepped back and smiled a big smile at their companion ... and traded partners. Now they were with the opposite partners as to what they had been with in the airplane. Once again ... another round of long amorous embraces and deep, deep kisses. Christie was transfixed. "My *goodness!*" slipped from her lips.

Round three! They traded partners *again*. The two girls smiled, embraced, and locked lips with each other, while the two guys did the same thing. Once again, a longer, even more ardent round of trading tongues and intimate caresses followed, only this time when the squeezes and hugs and kisses ended, the two women kept their arms around each other, said goodbye to the guys, and walked off in one direction, while the men departed hand-in-hand in the other direction.

Christie's eyes were as big as saucers as she looked back at me and whispered "Eeeeeuuuuwww!"

The collared-and-frocked preacher (*denomination unknown - I didn't ask*) was my only passenger to Hoonah, a predominantly native community about 20 minutes west of Juneau, so we chatted as I walked him out to the airplane. I'd just loaded quite a bit of baggage for him, so I presumed he was planning to be in Hoonah for awhile.

"Why are you going to Hoonah?" I asked. I knew he didn't live there, because his baggage tags listed an address in the South 48, many hundreds of miles away.

"I'm being led on a mission," he answered.

"Led?"

"Yes. I'm being led on this mission to Hoonah by Frog." He pulled a carved wooden frog about six inches long out of his pocket and held it out for me to see.

"That frog is taking you to Hoonah on a mission?"

"Yes."

*You would* think *that I'd learn to keep my mouth shut, but ...*

"I hope you'll pardon me for saying so," I said, "but it looks to me like you're taking the frog to Hoonah, not the other way around."

It was pretty quiet for the rest of the trip.

Skagway Air Service does a tremendous amount of tourism-related business every season. Skagway is a tourist town, and gets close to million visitors every summer, many of whom want to do something in an airplane.

However, when Labor Day arrives, Skagway rolls up the sidewalks, nails plywood over the windows, and people leave town in droves.

Before they go, though, SkagAir throws an end-of-the-season hangar party, a barbecue/beerbust/thank-you party for all and sundry who've made the past season a financial success.

I was still flying one season when the party took place, and had a flight to Skagway, followed by a leisurely deadhead to Juneau, so I stopped at the SkagAir hangar and had a barbecued beef sandwich and a cold can of pop.

As I walked back toward my airplane awhile later a voice hailed me. "Hey, Cap'n Bob, are you going to Juneau? Can we ride along?" It was one of our "new" seasonal pilots, a young fellow in his mid-twenties. He had a girl on each arm, and I recognized them both as counter agents from Juneau (*not from Haines Airways, by the way*).

"Sure, come along," I replied. "I'm deadheading anyway, so I'd enjoy some company."

"Well," he said, "You won't really be enjoying our company, because we're going to sit in back, and we don't want you to turn around during the flight."

The two girls just grinned and snuggled closer to him. It was obvious they'd all three enjoyed more beer than barbecue, and now were feeling amorous.

"Whatever," I said, "but I'm on my way right now." They ran over and climbed in the back seat, and I taxied out and took off for Juneau.

A Cherokee is a noisy machine, and I had a headset on, but every once in awhile I heard a shriek or a giggle or a high-pitched squeal from the back. I had absolutely no interest in being a witness to their back-seat gymnastics, so I didn't turn around, but when we got to Juneau 45 minutes later it was plain to see that the Mile High Club had just initiated three new members.

I had another charter from Haines to Hoonah one day. Two married couples, missionaries of some kind, wanted to fly to Hoonah where they were going to "convert the natives" (*their words, definitely not mine*). I was waiting next to 36 Romeo when they drove up in their van and started unloading stuff. Boxes of stuff, bags of stuff, rolls of stuff, suitcases, all kinds of stuff, all carefully packed and neatly labeled.

One couple was in their mid-fifties, and the other in their mid-twenties. I think the younger woman was the daughter of the older couple, but it could have been the young man was their son, I don't remember for sure, but in any case they were related.

They had lots of baggage, but it really wasn't very heavy, and a lot of it would squash, so I kept loading it aboard, just making sure that I had four open seats for the people. We got it all loaded, so I said, "OK, let's get aboard and head for Hoonah."

The day was "one of the few" in Southeast Alaska. The sky was a brilliant blue, the wind was absolutely calm, and there wasn't a ripple on the ocean or a cloud in the sky. The weather was fantastic.

The older man turned to me and said "We'd like to pray for good weather and the success of this flight before we go. Would you kneel with us in a time of prayer?"

"No, I don't think I will," I said, "but thanks for the invitation anyway. I'll just go ahead and preflight the airplane."

The four of them kneeled in a circle next to the airplane; the older man raised both hands, and began to pray in a loud voice. He went on for several minutes, praying that the weather would be good, their mission would be a success, they'd have enough food to eat, their heathen pilot wouldn't crash and kill them all, etc., etc., etc.

The other three just kneeled silently there on the taxiway, hands joined and heads bowed, until the older man finished. Then they all said "Amen" and got up and walked over to the plane, ready to go at last.

It was a beautiful flight. We were able to go direct, so we were up above the mountain tops, and could see Glacier Bay, Mount Fairweather, and parts of the Juneau Icecap. It was spectacular, and just as smooth as silk. The older fellow sat up front with me, but didn't seem to be noticing the fantastic scenery we were traversing. He kept his eyes closed a lot, and seemed to be moving his lips.

We landed in Hoonah, unloaded all their gear, and confirmed that they would call when they were ready to be picked up.

A week or so later Midge told me my morning schedule was to fly the 6 a.m. scheduled flight to Juneau, and then go over to Hoonah to pick up some charter passengers for Haines. The weather that morning was typical Southeast Alaska weather - low overcast, winds gusting to 40 knots, and heavy rain. The ceiling and visibility were both pretty pathetic, but it was still flyable.

When I got to Hoonah I found the four missionaries impatiently waiting for me, standing outside the terminal building in the downpour. Their stuff was scattered all over the place, some packed in boxes and containers, but quite a bit of it just laying around loose, almost like it had been thrown out of the back of a moving pickup truck. Everything they had was soaking wet, and the people looked like they had just been rescued from a boating disaster. I don't think I've ever seen four people look so miserable.

They started cramming their things in every nook and cranny of the airplane, oblivious to the pouring rain. I supervised to make sure they didn't load us out of balance, and when everything was aboard they started scrambling into the plane.

I couldn't resist ... I tried, I really did, but I just *couldn't* resist ...

"Wait a minute!" I commanded. All four of them stopped in their tracks and then edged toward me a little bit. I looked at the older man, then up at the stormy sky, and quietly asked, "Don't you think you should pray for good weather and the safety of the flight?"

He looked at me for one long second, one hand resting on the wind-shaken wingtip, raindrops dripping off his nose and chin, and then said "Let's just get the H--- *out* of here!" and climbed in the back of the airplane.

My lone passenger early one morning was a fairly attractive brunette in a short skirt, blouse, jacket and high heels. I didn't recognize her at all, so figured she was from out-of-town and just passing through. She had one suitcase, which I stowed in the back.

I had to get into the airplane first, and got settled while she carefully climbed up on the wing. She took off her jacket and tossed it into the back seat, and then bent over to climb into the right front seat, providing confirmation that she was bra-less.

I turned and looked away while she maneuvered herself into the seat, and then had her close the door and buckle her seat belt.

She made some comment about how she hoped I wasn't offended by her dress. I told her that how she dressed was none of my affair, and went about getting us up in the air and on our way.

Once we were airborne she dropped all pretense and said, "I'll bet you'd like to see some more, wouldn't you? I'll bet I can make you feel really good," and started to unbutton her blouse.

I was flabbergasted for a few seconds, by which time she had three or four buttons undone. Good grief!

"You might as well put your clothes back on," I said. "I'm not interested, and even if I was, if I take my hands off this wheel, this airplane will nose over and crash." I demonstrated by releasing the wheel and surreptitiously pressing the left rudder pedal, so the airplane skidded and lifted one wing.

Her eyes got wide and she asked, "Are you sure?"

"Yes ma'm." I replied, "I'm very sure."

When we got to Juneau I walked her in and handed her suitcase to her.

"I'll bet you're at least a little bit sorry it didn't work out, aren't you?" she asked plaintively.

"No ma'm, I'm not a bit sorry. Have a nice day."

Jerrold and his family arrived in town a few years after we did. He was fairly short, but had a sort of charismatic presence, dark wavy hair, and piercing blue eyes. His wife was a very pretty woman, always dressed in the latest style. His son, taller than Jerrold by several inches, was in high school, and his daughter, cute as a button, was in junior high.

Jerrold and his family were missionaries, too, "bringing the Good News to Southeast Alaska!" (again, his words, not mine). I don't remember what denomination they were, but somewhere in the southern U.S. some "foreign missions" board was supporting Jerrold and his family in their Alaskan efforts.

I got acquainted with Jerrold through flying. He had a fairly new private pilot's certificate, and pilots just naturally "find" each other, at least here in Alaska. We visited over coffee a few times, and had a few hangar flying sessions through that first winter, but Jerrold's flying experience was so limited that we soon ran out of things to discuss.

Jerrold didn't seem to be making much progress in spreading the Good News either. He had no local congregation, and didn't hold regular services anywhere that I knew of. Maybe he was concentrating on making converts one at a time. I don't know.

The following spring I ran into Jerrold at the post office one day, and the first thing he said was "Hi, you ought to come out to the airport and see my new airplane." He went on to tell me he had just acquired a Cessna 180, "in really nice shape."

A day or two later I went out to the airport to visit Ernie, and sure enough, there was a nifty looking silver Cessna 180 tied down in the parking area. Jerrold's car was alongside, so I ambled over to see his new airplane.

Jerrold was polishing the inside of the windshield when I walked up, and he jumped out of the cockpit to greet me. He gave me the walk-around tour, as proud as could be of his new airplane, and I didn't blame him. It was a *very* nice aircraft.

He then reached inside and grabbed a fairly big metal object. He held it out to me and exclaimed, "See! I've even got a new Bible for my airplane." Sure enough, it was a big Bible, the kind you see preachers reading out of up in the front of a church, and it had thick aluminum covers.

"I had it especially made for the airplane. This way I don't have to worry about it getting damaged if it gets tossed around in the back of the plane while I'm on my mission flights," and to demonstrate his point he took the Bible and tossed it about six feet into the back of the aircraft. It hit the floor with a resounding crash. "See," he said with a big smile, "no damage."

Yes, that was a pretty impressive demonstration, all right. It certainly made a big impression on me. After the dust settled I asked, "So, you're planning to do mission flights?"

"That's right. I told my mission board that I needed an airplane to carry God's Word to all the villages and settlements in Southeast. I want to go to Angoon and Tenakee, Kake and Pelican, Elfin Cove, all sorts of places like that, so the mission board bought me this airplane, and the Bible too."

"Well Jerrold, that's pretty neat. There's only one problem that I can see."

"Oh, what's that?" he asked.

"This is a wheel plane, and none of those places you mentioned have an airstrip."

He thought for a few seconds, and then said "Well, they probably will have eventually."

We get a lot of visitors in Southeast. Most are just tourist types, but there are also quite a few "professional" people or "business" people. Most tourists are pretty laid back and relaxed, but the other types are often wound tight. They have places to go and things to do, are tightly scheduled, and don't have time to "fool around," so this following scenario occurs fairly regularly in Southeast. The only change is the actual person involved, and it's almost invariably their first trip to Alaska.

Here's the scenario - the weather is absolutely horrid! Juneau tower says the official conditions are "200 ft. ceiling and a quarter mile visibility in rain and fog." Alaska Airlines with their super-duper IFR-equipped kerosene queen *might* make it in, but there isn't a propeller turning anywhere else. Even the seagulls are walking, and they're being extra careful.

A business-suit-and-briefcase type *(BS&B)* walks up to the air taxi ticket counter and says "I'd like a seat on your 2 p.m. flight to Haines."

Joann or one of the other girls politely says "I'll be happy to sell you ticket, sir, but I have to tell you that our 2 p.m. flight is presently on a weather hold."

"Does that mean it won't be leaving for Haines on time?" asks the BS&B.

"Yes sir, I'm afraid it does. The weather is too bad for us to fly right now."

The BS&B looks a little frustrated, picks up his brief case, and walks 30 feet down the line to the counter of another air taxi company. The girl there says she will be happy to accommodate him on her 2:15 flight to Haines, but "we are on a weather hold right now."

All the air taxi companies that serve Haines have adjacent counters in the Juneau terminal building, so the BS&B only has to move a few more feet before he is standing in front of his third ticket agent, a young woman who most definitely can get him on their 2:30 flight to Haines, except "our departure time is actually indefinite right now, as the weather is down and we can't fly."

The men and women who work as ticket agents are chosen for their charm, tact and winning personalities. They are often amazing at soothing ruffled feathers.

However, the BS&B also knows a few things, and he's not finished yet, so he goes back to the first air taxi counter and demands, "Well, if your scheduled flight isn't going, I'd like to charter!"

Duh!

The word spreads that there is a BS&B "shopping" out front, and often at this point a frustrated pilot will enter the picture. This pilot is frustrated because he can't fly due to the weather, and pilots are *not* necessarily hired for their charm, tact, or winning personalities. They're chosen because they are experienced and can be trusted to get an airplane and its passengers safely from point A to point B.

"Say, my friend, how many widgets is your life worth today?" this pilot might ask the BS&B.

"Errr, ahh ... pardon me?"

"Well, I assume you need to get to Haines right away to sell widgets or some such thing. If we leave now, on a schedule flight *or* a charter, we're definitely going to crash and all be killed. I'm just curious to know how many widgets you figure your life is worth?"

*By their second or third trip to Southeast Alaska, most of the BS&Bs have this weather thing figured out. They provide plenty of extra "weather" time in their schedules, relax a little, and enjoy their trips. They come to realize that even the down times can be rewarding experiences.*

One summer I kept track of the all the different nationalities I flew out of Haines. I'm sure I missed some, but the list included folks from Germany, Switzerland, South Africa, Italy, Mexico, China, France, Holland, Australia, New Zealand, Hungary, England, Israel, Japan, Canada, Sweden and of course, the US. At least seventeen different nationalities passed through our tiny isolated Southeast Alaska community of 2,000 people.

I thought Doris Bell was going to do me in one summer. She and her husband Clyde own two businesses in Haines. Clyde sells fresh and frozen seafood out of his shop in the old fire hall and Doris has a mercantile store right next door.

Back in the '80s, soon after Haines Airways got off the ground (*there's another one of those awful puns!*) Doris decided that Haines needed a coffee shop, so they set aside part of Clyde's storefront to serve coffee and pastries and hired their high school-aged niece, La-Zell Ahrens, to run the enterprise.

Haines had no bakery at the time (*why else would there be a need for a coffee shop?*), so Doris made arrangements with Fred Meyers, a large Juneau chain store with their own bake shop, to deliver four big boxes of assorted fresh-baked pastries, along with 20 pounds of freshly ground coffee, to the airport every morning.

I almost always had the early flight from Haines to Juneau, and then usually flew the return flight to Haines. Every single 7:00 a.m. departure for Haines that summer included these four boxes of pastries, just out of the oven, and the fresh coffee. For an hour I had to endure the tantalizing smell of all those goodies, and couldn't touch one. I had to load them into the airplane, fly them to Haines, transfer them into a company van, and then deliver them to Doris's coffee shop.

By the time I got there I'm sure my tongue was hanging out to my knees.

After my seventh or eighth delivery Doris said one morning, "Bob, why don't you have a doughnut and a cup of coffee before you leave?"

"Why, thanks, Doris. I think I might be able to spare just a couple of minutes."

# Chapter Twenty Three
## MORE OOPS!

The weather that June morning was just plain ugly! Throughout the whole Lynn Canal the ceiling was down to minimums, there was rain and fog and visibility was really poor.

I had flown down from Haines to Juneau early in the morning, and now an hour later I was headed back towards Haines with two passengers. We got out of the control zone and across Auke Bay with no problems, although it was marginal flying.

Once I got around Lena Point there is a relatively straight beach all the way to Berners Bay, so I eased out to the left until I could just still see the beach, slowed down to about 115 mph, dropped a notch of flaps, and slowly flew north along the shoreline. I wanted to stay as far off the beach as I could and still see it, so if I had to turn around I could turn into the beach and maintain visual reference to the shoreline. Turning away from visual references in fog is a good way to get vertigo and spin into the water.

I flew along past Tee Harbor and Eagle Beach, and as I came up abeam Gull Island, a tiny island about two-and-a-half miles offshore, I caught a glimpse of a landing light. It looked like there was a plane circling Gull Island at about 400 feet.

The light came around again, so I keyed the mike and said "Aircraft circling Gull Island, are you OK?"

This breathless voice came back immediately "Where are you?" and even more plaintively "Where am I?"

"Oh boy!" I thought. "I'll bet it's some new summer pilot who's gotten himself lost and is afraid to turn loose of the only land he can see."

"Where are you trying to go?" I asked.

"Haines." came the reply.

"Okay," I said. "I'm headed there too. I just passed you, so I'm going to turn around and come back, and then come past you again. When I do, you hook on behind me and we'll go to Haines together. Do you have a passenger in the front seat with you?"

"Yes, I have three passengers." (*I'll bet those were three un-happy people by that time.*)

"Alright, you concentrate on flying the airplane, and tell your front-seater to watch for me. When he sees me, he'll tell you, and you can spot me and drop in behind, OK?"

"Roger."

I did a slow turn into the beach and flew back south couple of miles. Then I turned back north again, easing out towards Gull Island so I could spot the other plane once more. When I saw him I turned towards Gull, using it as a visual reference, and timing myself so I would pop up close to the other plane when we were both going the same northerly direction.

I told him where I was, what I was doing, and where I should be in reference to his aircraft, and in just a few seconds I heard him say "I've got you!"

"Good deal. Pull in behind me and keep me in sight. I'm slowed down, cruising at 115 mph indicated, and I've got one notch of flaps down. Don't get too close, but don't lose sight of me."

I eased over toward the beach again, and he tagged along all the way to Haines. It didn't get any better, but it didn't get any worse, either, so we made it fine, although he *was* a little pale when we landed.

I'll bet when he writes a book, this story will come under the heading "I Learned About Flying From That."

Ron Smith and I were on a cross-country training flight in 99 Charlie. He had recently purchased the airplane from Ernie and me, and was working towards his private pilot's license. We were doing cross-country flights, and had been to Skagway and Juneau already that morning. Gustavus was to be our last stop. Then we'd do some navigation problems around the Sisters Island VOR and head back to Haines.

It was winter, and we'd had quite a bit of snow during the past few days, but I was positive the Gustavus runway would be plowed. We would have to be careful though, because the sky was overcast, the light was very dull, and depth perception could be tricky, especially in the snow.

We had quite a surprise waiting for us when we arrived at GST. The entire airport was covered by low fog. We hadn't encountered fog anywhere else, but Gustavus had a little pancake, several hundred feet thick, covering both runways and the surrounding buildings.

As we circled I realized two things. First, the fog didn't go all the way to the ground. There appeared to be fifty to seventy-five feet of clear air underneath the fog. Second, we could just barely make out the approach end of Runway 1, the runway the slight breeze favored.

Ron and I looked the situation over very carefully, and I asked him "What do you think, Ron? Could you put it right on the end of Runway 1 and land under the fog?"

"I think so" he said, and proceeded to enter a right downwind for Runway 1. He announced his downwind for Runway 1, right base for Runway 1, and turn-to-final for Runway 1 on the CTAF, and did a good job of ending up at the very threshold of Runway 1 for a landing.

Something didn't feel quite right though, so I said "Increase your power, Ron, don't set it down yet."

Under that blanket of fog all depth perception was gone. We could see. In fact, we could see all the way under the fog and out the other side, but with the flat light we couldn't distinguish any details about the runway surface.

We were about a third of the way down the runway when I saw moose tracks cutting diagonally across the runway. "Go around, Ron. Go Around!"

Ron firewalled it and headed for the clear air on the other side of the fog layer ... and buzzed the road grader that was busy plowing the intersecting runway. We literally went right in front of the cab, about 20 feet off the ground, and must have frightened the operator half to death.

As we crossed the intersecting runway I could see the distinct difference between "plowed" and "not plowed." The runway we had intended to land on had two feet of snow covering it. Had we touched down we'd have crashed instantly.

I never have understood why the grader driver, who had a radio in his grader, or the air taxi base on the field, didn't come on and tell us that Runway 1 was unusable. However, in the end it was our (*my!*) responsibility. The Alaska Flight Information Publication clearly says "Runway 1-19 not maintained Oct. 15 -April 30." I just hadn't done all my homework.

We didn't go around and land on Runway 28. We flew back to Haines, went to the bakery, and discussed the lesson we'd both learned over coffee and doughnuts.

The FlyCruise flight that night was huge! There must have been 35 air taxi aircraft squeezed into the Skagway airport parking area.

The folks in charge were competent and efficient, and loaded planes were buzzing out of Skagway and climbing for the Icecap every 30 to 45 seconds.

It was a beautiful evening, so the planes fanned out all over the Icecap, each pilot following his or her favorite route, or maybe going to some part of the Icecap they hadn't seen before, or perhaps just wandering around.

In any case, each plane would eventually head for the Mendenhall Towers, descend the Mendenhall Glacier, contact Juneau Tower at the base of the glacier, and be sequenced for landing.

As usual, many of the planes arrived at Mendenhall Towers at roughly the same time. As each plane started to descend down the glacier, the pilot's job was to locate the plane immediately ahead of him, make some space between, and identify the plane just ahead by "N" number, all by the time he or she reached the base of the glacier.

Finding and spacing wasn't too hard, but you had to pay close attention on the radio to pick up the "N" number.

The first aircraft to reach the terminus of the glacier might report something like this: "Juneau Tower, SkagAir 31 Xray, Mendenhall Lake for a landing, FlyCruise."

Mendenhall Glacier and Mendenhall Lake. Skagway FlyCruise flights descended the glacier from the Juneau Icefield and reported here for landing at Juneau International Airport.
Juneau, Alaska – Summer, 1995

Juneau Tower now knew that the FlyCruise circus had come to town, and they were going to be inundated with small aircraft for the next 20 minutes. The tower would respond with landing instructions for 31 Xray - on this particular night a very pleasant female voice replied "31 Xray, enter right downwind for Runway 26, you're cleared to land."

Three One Xray didn't say anything else. He just clicked his mike button twice to acknowledge the tower's instructions. He knew what to do, and besides ... the aircraft right behind him had now identified him by "N" number, and was reporting "Juneau Tower, Wings 23 Bravo in trail behind 31 Xray."

The tower acknowledges - "Roger 23 Bravo. Continue in sequence"

And the third plane in line says "Tower, HainesAir 81 Whiskey in trail behind 23 Bravo"

"Roger 81 Whiskey, continue."

"Tower, SkagAir 15 Poppa trailing 81 Whiskey"

"One five Poppa, continue"

Etc. Etc. Etc. Do you see how it goes? Bing, Bing, Bing ... rapid fire, with 35 airplanes pouring down the glacier and into the landing pattern just a few seconds apart.

Now, about four air taxis into this nice orderly procession, comes a fly, a huge aluminum fly, in the ointment. Enter an Alaska Airlines 737 jet coming in from the north.

"Juneau Tower, Alaska Flight 75, fifteen miles out, canceling IFR, request straight in Runway 8." (*Runway 8 is the opposite end of Runway 26. The airline pilot wants to land head on into the stream of air taxis.*)

"Alaska Flight 75, Juneau Tower, roger canceling IFR, Runway 26 is the current runway."

"Tower, Flight 75 is requesting straight in on 8." (*This jet pilot is sounding pretty insistent.*)

"Seventy Five, Tower. I have many small aircraft coming down the glacier for 26." (*There's a reason I don't want to put you straight in. It's going to mess up the traffic pattern royally.*)

Throughout this whole conversation air taxi aircraft are pouring down the glacier, and trying to get a word in edgeways while this heavy iron driver argues with the tower.

"Tower, Flight 75. Do you realize how much extra fuel it costs my company to fly 10 miles down the Channel, and then come back just to land on 26. I'm requesting straight in on Runway 8." (*There, I've played my ace. I want what I want when I want it, and you can't deny me!*)

"Flight 75, Tower. Roger your request for straight in Runway 8. Hold over ASORT intersection until Runway 8 becomes available." (*ASORT intersection is a place on the IFR approach where two radio beams come together. It's out in the aeronautical boonies, so to speak, so the lady in the tower has just said "OK, Bozo. I'm tired of messing with you. You can just fly your big important airplane around in circles out there in the ozone until I'm good and ready to let you land ... on Runway 8."*)

Of course all the air taxi pilots could hear this whole conversation, and you can bet there were many big grins as we looked straight down the runway and saw Flight 75 circling far off in the distance. The controller kept him out there for a good 15 minutes, until every last FlyCruise plane had landed and taxied clear. Then she cleared him to land ... straight in on Runway 8!

Oops!

Speaking of Alaska Airlines, Flight 71 had just departed Juneau's Runway 26 and was climbing through 2,000 feet over Coghlan Island when something hit the pilot's windshield so hard that it cracked it. The pilot was startled out of his wits, but kept things under control. A pressurized airliner can't legally continue flying with a cracked windshield so he aborted the flight and returned to Juneau.

When the aircraft was safely on the ground mechanics examined the windshield and found fish slime all over the glass and frame.

Apparently an eagle had been carrying a fish somewhere above 2,000 feet, and the jet frightened it, causing the eagle to drop its fish. The jet then ran into the fish, suffering a broken windshield in the process.

The next day the Juneau Empire's banner headline read "EAGLES 1, JETS O"

Oops! (*This story could possibly be apocryphal. It was related to me by a trustworthy source, but if it's not true, please don't spoil it for me, because I really enjoy the story.*)

Back in the early days of Haines Airways, the Haines airport was pretty primitive. It was a chip-coated strip, with two ramshackle hangars and no fueling facilities whatsoever.

When I started flying for Haines Airways, right after they started operations, one of the first rules I learned was "fuel up whenever you have the opportunity." Fuel was only available in Skagway and Juneau, so whenever I flew to one of those places the first thing I did was fill up. I never knew where the schedule would take me next, and I might have to fly four or five hours before I'd get back to a fueling facility again.

I had a Skagway FlyCruise flight one night, so when I flew over to Skagway the first thing I did was stop at the pumps and fill up, all four tanks, right to the top.

When the buses brought our passengers out, Darlene, the Fly-Cruise coordinator, would get all the passengers out of the buses and onto the apron. She would then call out a pilot's name and hand him or her a piece of paper with their passenger's names and weights, luggage weight, and total weight. The pilot would add his own weight and fuel weight, and then go over to the group, call out his passenger's names, lead them to his airplane, load up and take off for Juneau, via the Icecap.

Darlene called my name, smiled as she handed me my passenger list, and said, "You've got a family of five. They didn't want to be split up. It's a couple and their three daughters."

I looked at my manifest and just about fainted. The couple and their three daughters listed weights of 355, 335, 295, 280, and 265, for a total of 1,530 lb., plus 100 lb. of baggage.

I should explain here that a Cherokee Six, depending on year of manufacture and installed equipment, has a useful load of approximately 1,500 lb. That means that the *total* passenger, pilot, luggage, *and fuel* weight is not supposed to exceed this amount, and I had just pumped eighty four gallons of aviation fuel (*at six pounds per gallon*) into my airplane.

My fuel weighed 504 lb., I weighed 185 lb., and my passengers alone weighed 1,530 lb.! I turned to Darlene and said "They've *got* to split up!"

"Hey, I'm sorry. We tried, but they absolutely refuse to be separated."

"OK, send them on a bigger plane," I said.

"There's nothing bigger than a Cherokee Six going on FlyCruise tonight."

Dang!

"Well, I absolutely can't take their luggage. They can mail it home as far as I'm concerned."

She replied "I'll find somewhere else to stow their baggage, if you can just take the people."

I went over to the group and called their names, and five giants walked toward me. They ranged from 6'2" to maybe 6'7," and were all what we might call "really ample" people.

I walked them over to the airplane, sorted them out so the weight would be balanced, and loaded them aboard. I could hear the airplane groaning under the weight. They were all so big that none of them could get their seat belts around them. I only had one seatbelt extender, so I didn't even mention fastening seat belts. We were jammed in so tight no one would be able to move anyway.

The Skagway runway is 3,700 feet long, and points out over the ocean. If (and it was a BIG if) I could get airborne, there wasn't anything higher than sea level between Skagway and Juneau.

Full power and 3,000 feet later the Cherokee broke ground and staggered into the air ... but not by much. She very slowly climbed to fifty feet or so, and that was pretty much it.

I was supposed to take these folks to Juneau via the Icecap. In other words, climb to 4,500 feet and show them the icefield, glaciers and mountaintops. By the time I got to Sawmill Creek, our normal turnoff to head up onto the Icecap, I was showing just over a hundred feet altitude. Under normal circumstances I would have been at around three thousand feet.

"Folks, we were supposed to climb up to mountaintop level, but it's such a nice calm evening I think I'd like to just stay down low and see what we can see along the beaches. There should be some wildlife out at this time of evening. How does that sound to you?"

I gave a sigh of relief as they all smiled and nodded.

Eighteen miles down the canal I slowly milked off the notch of flaps I'd been carrying. A little further on I eased back just a tiny bit from full power and found I could maintain altitude with climb power, but not with cruise power.

When I got to Eagle Beach forty minutes later, I'd burned enough gas that climb power was giving me around 25 feet per minute of climb, so when I reached Lena Point and entered the Juneau control zone I had enough altitude to make it through the Cut.

I didn't want to try slowing down at all, so I crossed the runway threshold without ever coming back on the throttle, and landed doing 140 mph. It took nearly 5,000 feet of runway to stop. Just like the big jets, eh?

❖

I brought a planeload of mail and freight from Juneau to Haines one day, and entered the downwind leg for Runway 8 in the standard manner, announcing my arrival on the CTAF.

No one was in the pattern ahead of me, but I noticed what looked like a Piper Cub circling down low over Murphy Flats across the river off to my left. I assumed the pilot was searching for moose or bears on the flats.

As I reached mid-field on my downwind leg, I saw that the Cub had quit circling and was headed directly for the approach end of Runway 8, still very close to the ground, and perpendicular to the runway. Was he going to enter the landing pattern, or was he going to try to slip in ahead of me?

"Piper Cub approaching Haines over the river. Are you intending to land?"

No answer. Maybe he doesn't have a radio.

"Haines traffic, 36 Romeo turning right base for 8. Piper Cub, what are your intentions?"

No answer, but he's still heading for the runway. I noticed that a big twin-engine Piper Chieftain had fired up and was slowly taxiing toward the departure end of runway 8 also.

"Three Six Romeo turning final for runway 8 in Haines."

By now I'd recognized the Cub. It's belonged to a young local man who had a reputation for "forgetting" proper procedures pretty regularly.

The Cub was getting very close to the runway, still at 50 feet altitude, when he turned hard left, straightened out for just a second, and then made a steep 180 degree right turn back towards the runway. He was going to cut right in front of me and land.

In the meantime the Chieftain had taxied up just short of the runway and was doing his runup.

I announced, "Haines Traffic, Three Six Romeo, short final for 8."

The Cub flared out, landed right on the very end of the runway, braked hard, and immediately turned left to exit on the first taxiway ... and found the Chieftain sitting there, completely blocking his exit. The Cub was sitting high and dry, crossways on the runway threshold, with me on *very* short final right behind him.

I'm afraid a lesson is about to be delivered!

"Back up! There's a plane on short final right behind me!" Aha! The Cub *does* have a radio!

The Chieftain pilot was completely astonished, and rightly so. This little Cub materialized in front of him out of nowhere, with other "normal" traffic on short final, and the Cub now wants him to "back up."

"Back up? What do you think this thing is? A pickup truck?"

By this time I was right down on top of the Cub and it's time to deliver the lesson:

I shout into the radio "THREE SIX ROM-EE-OO, GOING AR-OU-NN-D!" and go to full throttle and low pitch right over the top of the Cub, about 10 feet over his head. The noise must have been *tremendous* in that little fabric airplane.

Oops!

I went around the pattern again, and as I turned base on my second landing attempt, I saw the young pilot's pickup leaving the airport, so I didn't get a chance to see him face-to-face right away. I noticed he was pretty stand-offish for the next few weeks, even though I never mentioned the incident.

For the rest of the summer, whenever I'd meet the Chieftain pilot, he'd give me a big grin and quietly say "Going Ar-ou-nn-d," or "Back Up!" and we'd both laugh.

The young man went on to get his commercial and instrument ratings, and flew for an Alaskan air taxi company for awhile. I was talking to his boss at the Juneau Airport a year or two later, and asked about him.

"He's my most dependable, trustworthy pilot. Everything he does is done *exactly* by the book. I really hate to lose him. He's moving up to fly for one of the mid-sized commuter airlines in the Northwest."

# Chapter Twenty Four
## JUST PLANE (sic) FUN

Airplanes can be a lot of fun, partly because they operate in three dimensions instead of just two, but there's a world of difference between having responsible fun in an airplane, and just screwing around.

One of our "responsible fun" procedures occurred almost every time any of us would deadhead from Skagway to Haines. Sometimes, such as when returning from Nature Tour flights, there might be four or five of us. Other times we'd be alone.

We'd leave Skagway and fly directly to the radio relay tower on Ripinski Ridge above Haines. To clear the ridge we'd have to be at somewhere around 2,300 feet altitude. When we crossed the ridge, we would immediately be looking down an extremely steep wooded mountainside, almost directly above the Haines Airport.

We could easily see any traffic within five miles of the airport, and *if the pattern was empty,* we'd pull back the throttle and push over into a steep 1,500 foot descent to pattern altitude *(800 feet),* and broadcast on the CTAF "Haines Traffic, 36 Romeo, Ripinski Relay Tower, descending for a midfield crossover and right downwind for runway 8." If another airplane was present they would immediately radio "81 Whiskey, in trail," and so on.

There might be four or five airplanes, one after another, skimming down the mountainside, across the middle of the airfield, and into a very tight circular pattern, simultaneously slowing and descending with the object being to arrive at the runway threshold having just reached landing speed and in landing configuration, touch down smoothly, and roll off at the first intersection just as the airplane behind you touched down. It was essentially a variation on the standard military overhead approach.

It was great fun in the air, impressive to watch from the ground, and involved no potential hazards to anyone.

Denise, my older daughter, likes airplanes. We both really enjoyed going out together so she could fly 99 Charlie. For awhile I thought she might take lessons and get her pilot's license, but she ended up getting her dispatcher's certification and working for Conoco-Phillips company airlines. She now lives in Anchorage, scheduling and dispatching three or four charter jet flights a day to ConocoPhillips' North Slope oil fields.

❖

Cheryl, one of our dispatchers in Haines, called me out of the back room one morning and said "We've got a charter. This lady wants to fly around Haines today."

I turned to the nicely dressed middle-age lady standing on the other side of the counter and said "Good morning, ma'am. My name's Bob. I'll be your pilot today. Do you have anything specific you'd like to see, and how long would you like to be gone?"

"Yes, I have some very specific places to see, and I suspect you'll add more places as we go. We'll be gone for as long as it takes. I suspect it will take most of the day."

She motioned me over to our big aeronautical wall map of the area, and started to explain. She was a U.S. Census Bureau employee, and her job was to make sure the latest census didn't miss anyone. Therefore we were going to fly over all the remote areas of the Haines Borough, investigate any outlying cabins we found, and if there were signs of human habitation, she would find some way to reach those places and run the residents to ground so they could be interviewed and counted.

She had marked quite a few cabin sites on her maps, and I had been flying the area for several years so I added several more places to her inventory, and we would both keep our eyes peeled for other potential sites while we flew.

Cheryl put us in 808, a Cessna 182 with high wings and long range tanks, and away we went. We spent the entire day looking over the remotest areas of the borough. We flew low, following the riverbanks and beaches, and poked into every little valley, checking for buildings or smoke or any sign of human habitation.

When we'd see a cabin I'd circle low over it while the census agent looked carefully, often with binoculars, to see if it looked inhabited. If the building's door was open, or if it had broken windows we regarded it as uninhabited. In a couple of instances we circled for several minutes while she scanned for fresh tracks.

We worked our way from the upper Chilkoot Valley around into the Chilkat and Kelsoll Valleys, and all the way down Lynn Canal to Point Couverden and around to Excursion Inlet cannery, a straight-line distance of nearly 50 miles, but the way we went it was more like 350. We landed at XIP (yes, *Libby and Harry Rietz were there to meet us*) so the agent could check to see if all the cannery workers had been counted. While we were there the mess hall cooks fed us a delicious lunch, even though it was nearly mid-afternoon and the mess hall was supposed to be closed.

By late afternoon we had covered all the territory the bureau wanted covered, and were on our way back to Haines. She had three or four places that she felt she needed to explore on the ground, and I had one of the most enjoyable days of flying I'd ever had.

Several more really enjoyable flights, similar to the census flight, took place because the Alaska Dept. of Fish and Game wanted to troll for king salmon with an airplane.

Randy Erickson, the ADF&G fish biologist, was doing king salmon research in the early '90s. He wanted to know *exactly* which rivers, streams, creeks, or rivulets had spawning king salmon in them.

He put a fish wheel with a livebox in the Chilkat River at 7 Mile, and whenever the wheel captured a spawner king, Randy would implant a miniature waterproof battery-powered high frequency radio transmitter in the fish and turn it loose again. The king would continue on its way up the valley to whichever stream was its spawning stream, and periodically Randy would fly over the entire Chilkat Valley with a special radio set up that could detect the signal from the king salmon's transmitter. The signal was sometimes detectable from over a half mile away, depending on the water's depth.

Randy frequently chartered Haines Airways, specifically 808, the high wing Cessna 182, to do his "trolling" or fish finding, and I often drew the assignment to be his pilot. He would load his high frequency equipment into the plane and hook it up, and we'd be off for a couple of hours of low level "fishing." We would fly along a riverbank at six or seven hundred feet altitude until Randy got a "hit."

When a signal was detected, he'd ask me to circle and circle until he was absolutely certain of the fish's location. Sometimes the water was clear enough that we could actually spot the fish from the air. Each fish had been implanted with a transmitter with a slightly different frequency, so Randy could distinguish individual fish, and know whether it was "Henry" or "Helen" that we had "caught."

When an individual transmitter quit moving around, he would know the salmon had spawned and died, and he or one of his helpers would go in on foot to retrieve the transmitter. I understand they salvaged about 50%. The rest were either washed out to sea, or the bears either destroyed them or scattered them in the woods where they couldn't be found.

Except for the mandatory spin training that's required for a commercial license, I never had any formal aerobatic training, but I sure enjoyed those spins. The flight schools I attended in California and Arizona both used aerobatic Champion Citabrias for their spin training, but 99 Charlie was just as much fun to spin. I occasionally took a friend or family member along for a little "spin" in Charlie, but they never seemed to enjoy it as much as I did.

All of the Cherokees I flew were specifically prohibited from aerobatics. I wasn't about to see if the Piper engineers really knew what they were talking about, so my maneuvering in them was limited to steep turns and lazy eights.

Cheryl called me out of the back room in Haines one morning, saying "Cap'n Bob, come out here. I've got a surprise, and a GBT for you, in that order."

Standing at the counter were George and Haile Ball, father and stepmother of one of my closest old school friends. I had gone through both high school and college with their daughter Becky.

Becky's husband, Les Collins, had also been a classmate of ours all through school, and had been my roommate in college. I had been the best man at their wedding. They all still lived back in Michigan.

George and Haile had decided to visit Alaska, gotten my address from Les and Becky, and drove several hundred miles out of their way to see me, fly with me, and perhaps get a look at Glacier Bay. What a wonderful surprise!

The weather didn't look too cooperative, but Cheryl said we should give it a try, so I took George and Haile out to the airport, loaded them in 808, and looked for a way into Glacier Bay.

We tried the Davidson Glacier, we flew past the Rainbow Glacier, and went up the Tahkeen River, poking into every little valley that might possibly be open. Each of those valleys had their own glacier, coming down from the Glacier Bay icefield, but none of them were open at the top. We flew all the way up to and around the Tsirku Glacier, but ... no luck. Glacier Bay was closed!

I went down to 500 feet coming back down the Tahkeen valley, and on the way we saw several moose, a couple of brown bears, and a black wolf.

We were gone almost an hour, and had a beautifully scenic flight, but since we couldn't get in to Glacier Bay, Haines Airways refunded George and Haile's money.

Variety is the spice of life. On one busy day my logbook entry reads "Landed in HNS, JNU, GST, XIP, SKG, KAK, PBG, plus a GBT - 7.1 hrs." I visited eight different destinations in one day of flying.

In 1989 and '90 half the people in town were dreaming of becoming movie stars and Oscar winners. The Walt Disney movie *White Fang* was being filmed in and around Haines and Skagway, and many locals were hired as extras, doubles and go-fers. One local, Wendell Hales, was the stand-in for Ethan Hawke during his snowshoe sprint across a frozen lake. By the end of several consecutive takes, Wendell's tongue was definitely hanging out. Many Haines locals appear in the film *(if you know where to look)*, and several, including Aaron Hotch, Charlie Jimmy Sr., Cliff Fossman, and Irwin Sogge actually had speaking parts.

Haines Airways enjoyed some of the prosperity the movie company brought to town. It was always interesting to see what they would need next, almost always on an "emergency" basis. I flew movie stars and wolves, technicians and dog teams, dignitaries and supplies, and studio "rubber-neckers" regularly. Bart the Bear was too big for an air taxi, though, and had to come up on the Alaska state ferry.

The actual cast members, especially Klaus Maria Brandauer and Ethan Hawke, were the most enjoyable to fly, as was the director, Randal Kleiser. They all seemed to be regular down-to-earth folks. Some of the studio dignitaries were the worst, and the lower they were on the totem pole, the higher the opinion they seemed to have of themselves.

Juneau Ground cleared me to taxi to Runway 26, and at the same time cleared Alaska Airlines Flight 76, a Boeing 737, to do the same thing. Since I was smaller and nimbler, *and* knew what happens when you take off *behind* an airliner, I beat him to the taxiway and went on down to the very end of 26.

I switched to Juneau Tower and said "Tower, HainesAir 81 Whiskey, ready for takeoff," but tower said to hold short as there was an aircraft on a long straight-in approach. Landing aircraft always have the right-of-way. In the meantime Flight 76 taxied up behind me and stopped *really* close to my tail.

I glanced out toward the approach end of the runway, and saw that the aircraft on final was close to landing and so wouldn't be talking to the tower for a minute. I also knew Flight 76 had to be on tower frequency, so even though it was strictly against regulations I keyed my mike and said quietly but firmly, "If you touch me there I'll scream!"

Flight 76 keyed back, chuckling, and said, "Never fear, wee one. You're safe. By the way, where did you get that little spam can, anyway?"

"Our company has several of these." I said "We made them all ourselves out of the wreckage of one of Alaska Airlines' 737s."

The landing traffic swept by, and I could hear more laughter in the background as the tower came on and said "Alright, alright. Eight One Whiskey, taxi into position and hold."

I always carried an aluminum clipboard with me when I flew. It was made especially for pilots, and had an inch-thick storage box built into it. I carried my FLIP manual (*airport diagrams*), sunglasses and maybe a candy bar, or whatever other essentials I figured I might need for the day.

I went to a garage sale one day, and among all the goodies was a bright red 6" x 9" paperback book, with the title in big white block letters ..."Learn To Fly In Ten Easy Lessons."

Fifty cents later that gem was mine, and I don't think I ever enjoyed a book more, even though I don't remember ever reading a word of it. I kept it in my clipboard, and whenever I had a passenger who wanted to know if I was *sure* it would be safe to fly, or had a friend or acquaintance from Haines aboard, or just felt like stirring the pot, I would taxi out to the end of the runway, and make a big show out of getting my book out and referring to it, making sure, of course, that the passengers could clearly see the title first.

I heard lots of startled inhales, and a lot more genuine belly laughs.

# Chapter Twenty Five
## TRAGEDY NEAR GUSTAVUS

Barb Shallcross, co-owner of Haines Airways and a fellow air taxi pilot, and I were sitting in the back room visiting between flights late one August afternoon when Midge came in and said "I've got two flights for you guys. I have a pickup for five backpackers in Gustavus coming back to Haines, and a GBT. Who wants what?"

Barb looked at me, and I said "Ladies first. You choose, and I'll take the other one."

Barb chose the Gustavus pickup, so I took the GBT.

Two hours later I was back in the office and Midge asked, "Did you hear anything from Barb while you were in Glacier Bay? I haven't heard from her since she departed Gustavus on her way back here."

An hour later Barb was reported overdue, and a search was launched. It was close to dark, but every air taxi operating in the area contributed search planes and personnel. When an airplane goes missing, the concept of "competitor" is firmly put aside. It's a fellow aviator that's in trouble, and nothing is spared to find them. U.S. Coast Guard helicopters and several private aircraft also participated.

Early the next day the search resumed, with dozens of aircraft combing the area between Gustavus and Haines.

Later that morning one of our own pilots found the wreckage of 75 Whiskey. It had flown full power into a mountainside at 4,000 feet elevation. It burned and was totally destroyed. There was no reasonable explanation, so the NTSB called it "pilot error."

The NTSB Accident Investigation Report (7) states:

AFTER DEPARTING THE GUSTAVUS AIRPORT, THE PILOT TURNED THE AIRCRAFT TOWARD EXCURSION INLET & AIR-FILED A VFR FLIGHT PLAN. AFTER THE FLIGHT PLAN WAS FILED, THERE WERE NO FURTHER RADIO TRANSMISSIONS FROM THE AIRCRAFT. A SEARCH WAS INITIATED, BUT HEAVY FOG, CLOUDS & DARKNESS HAMPERED THE SEARCH. WRECKAGE WAS FOUND THE NEXT MORNING, WHERE THE AIRCRAFT HAD CRASHED ON STEEP RISING TERRAIN IN A BOX CANYON AREA. IMPACT OCCURRED AT THE END OF A VALLEY THAT BEGAN NEAR EXCURSION INLET. ELEVATION OF THE CRASH SITE WAS APPROX.

4000 FT. TERRAIN IN THAT AREA ROSE TO ABOUT 4600 FT. TWO OTHER PILOTS THAT DEPARTED HAINES NEAR THE TIME OF THE ACCIDENT REPORTED THE CEILING WAS BROKEN TO OVERCAST AT ABOUT 4000 FT. REPORTEDLY, THE MOUNTAIN TOPS WERE OB-SCURED, BUT THE VISIBILITY BELOW THE CLOUDS WAS ABOUT 20 MI. THE PROP BLADES WERE FOUND WITH DEEP CHORDWISE SCARS & LEADING EDGE/ ROTATIONAL DAMAGE.

The National Transportation Safety Board determines the probable cause(s) of this accident as follows:

VFR FLIGHT BY THE PILOT INTO INSTRUMENT METEOROLOGICAL CONDITIONS (IMC), AND THE PILOT'S FAILURE TO MAINTAIN SUFFICIENT ALTI-TUDE AND/OR CLEARANCE FROM MOUNTAINOUS TERRAIN. FACTORS RELATED TO THE ACCIDENT WERE: THE ADVERSE WEATHER AND TERRAIN CON-DITIONS.

# Chapter Twenty Six
## STILL MORE OOPS!

It was just getting dark one Saturday evening, and I was headed back home to Haines from a FlyCruise. I was by myself, so decided I would fly home along the beach, at about 500 feet altitude, and see what I could see in the failing light.

I came around Sherman Point, halfway between Haines and Juneau, and just offshore lay a gillnetter *(commercial fishing boat)*. The commercial fishermen's open fishing period didn't start until the next day at noon, so I thought it was a little strange that this fellow would be out so far ahead of time. True, Sherman Point was a gillnetting "hotspot." It was the southern boundary of the Lynn Canal fishing area, and sockeye salmon milled around the point. A number of boats would show up here early tomorrow morning, but this guy was *way* early.

I passed almost directly above him, and as I did I saw his cork line stretched out between his boat and the shore. He had his net in the water, and was going to skim the cream during the dark of the night! I recognized the boat, so when I got closer to town I radioed the office and asked them to call ADF&G and tell them what I'd seen.

Early the next morning a fisheries patrol found the gillnetter in a little bight with his anchor down and his stabilizers out. The anchor and both stabilizers had brailers *(heavy net bags)* containing several hundred sockeyes tied to them.

Oops!

I was headed for Juneau at six in the morning. The weather was pretty good for a change, so I was cruising at 2,000 feet. As I crossed Berners Bay and approached Mab Island I thought I saw smoke coming from somewhere around Bridget Cove.

Queen Anne Tours had a big new rustic log lodge and tour ship dock in Bridget Cove. They ran dayboat tours up to Haines and Skagway, using a couple of hundred-foot boats. The lodge served as their terminal, office, and hospitality center. It was only used in the summer time, so the main part of the lodge was heated with a big fireplace.

I turned into the cove for a closer look, and saw that there was no longer a lodge there. There was still some open flame, but mostly it was just a pile of smoking ruins, and a big stone fireplace standing all by itself.

I called Juneau Radio (*flight service station*), told them about the Queen Anne building, and asked if they would call the Juneau Fire Department to see if the fire had been reported.

The Juneau Empire later reported that an employee had cleaned out the fireplace the previous evening after all the clients had left the building. He put the ashes in a cardboard box, and put the box out on the wooden deck with the rest of the trash containers.

Apparently there were still live coals in the ashes. The coals ignited the box, the box ignited the deck, and the deck ignited the building. The lodge couldn't be seen from the highway, and there's very little traffic along that road after midnight, so Queen Anne's building burned to the ground and no one saw it go.

Oops!

Here's another lesson learned during my time as a student at the University of Severe Aeronautical Experiences.

My schedule for the morning called for a 6:00 a.m. flight to Juneau, then a 7:00 a.m. trip to Hoonah, return to Juneau, and then a 9 o'clock return to Haines.

Ho hum! Another beautiful day here in Paradise. The weather was CAVU (*ceiling and visibility unlimited*) except for a few very faint wisps of cloud along the mountains around Haines. As I neared Juneau there were more wispy, almost foggy patches, and the visibility around the Juneau airport itself was down to 7 or 8 miles due to fog. I knew the sun would dissipate the fog before too long, and it wasn't enough of a problem to hinder flight operations at Juneau anyway.

I called Juneau FSS on the telephone and asked for current weather conditions in Hoonah, and got the discouraging report that Hoonah was presently "zero, zero, heavy fog." In other words, Hoonah was socked in tight, and I had nothing to do except sit around and be bored.

I knew a Wings of Alaska floatplane had just arrived from Pelican, and the pilot would have come past, or maybe even right over, Hoonah. I walked down to the Wings counter and asked to talk to the pilot that had just arrived from Pelican.

"What did Hoonah look like when you came by there?" I asked.

He replied, "It's beautiful out there. All that fog from this morning has burned off everywhere except in that bowl that the Hoonah airport is in. There's no wind, and the sun isn't quite high enough yet to shine right down into the bowl. Once the sun hits that fog it will dissipate right away. In fact, I wouldn't be surprised if it's not mostly gone now. I'll bet if you left here right now it would be totally clear by the time you got there."

I went back to our counter, phoned a flight plan in to the FSS, went out and took off to make the 20-minute flight to Hoonah.

Sure enough, there wasn't a cloud in the sky. Everything was as clear as a bell ... until I got to Hoonah.

The town of Hoonah is separated from the Hoonah airport by a low ridge. The fog had dissipated everywhere except in the bowl where the runway was located, so the entire airport was covered with thick fog, but even though it was only a couple of hundred feet thick there was no sign at all of the runway, parking apron, or terminal building, so there was still no hope of landing.

I flew off a little ways and orbited at 1,500 feet for a few minutes, then decided I'd fly down Port Frederick and check out Neka Bay and the Salt Chuck.

Twenty minutes later I was back over the Hoonah airport, and sure enough, the fog was slowly dissipating. I could see the first 50 yards of Runway 5 clearly, and I could just make out the shadow of the terminal building out to my left on the edge of the fog bank.

"Okay," I thought. "If I can make out the terminal building from this high up, that fog must be pretty thin. I'll bet I can set down on the clear end of the runway, and have enough visibility to see the centerline and edge markers, and follow the yellow brick road (*the common nickname for runway and taxiway centerlines*) right to the terminal parking area. By the time I unload my freight and collect my passengers, it will be clear enough to take off again."

I circled and set up a landing approach to touch down on the very end of Runway 5, dragged in low and slow, and hit the first five feet of pavement ... and was almost instantly enveloped in fog so thick I could barely make out my prop spinner. I could *not* see my wingtips. It was like flying into a bottle of milk.

I carefully braked, hoping that I would stay on the runway. I sensed that I'd stopped rolling, and hadn't heard any major crashes or felt any thumps, so I assumed I hadn't done any damage. Now all I had to do was hope that nobody else pulled the same boneheaded stunt and tried to land behind me.

I must have sat there for better than five minutes before my eyes got adjusted to the foggy atmosphere, and my rotating prop set up a little wind current. I finally made out the centerline, and realized that if I taxied just to the right of it, I could look straight down and see it as it went under my wing.

I slowly taxied along, and fairly soon came to a place where the yellow line curved off to the left. That had to be where we turn off to taxi to the terminal. I followed the curve and crept along for another couple of hundred yards. The fog began to thin out a little, and I could finally make out the terminal building just ahead.

I parked and went inside to talk to the local agent. "How in the world did you get in here?" she asked. "I haven't been able to see a thing all morning!"

"Piece o' cake" I replied.

But I had learned my lesson! I knew that the whole episode boiled down to one big ...

Oops!

"Hey you guys! Hurry up! This twin's landing with his gear up."

Several of us barreled out of the Skagway terminal, looked up the final approach path, and sure enough, there was a light twin-engine air taxi on short final, and his landing gear was still securely tucked up in his wings. There was absolutely nothing we could do, except stand and watch the show.

Seconds later the pilot flared and gently settled toward the runway - a beautiful landing so far, with the minor exception of no landing gear.

Lower and lower ... and the lights must have come on in the pilot's head, because both engines suddenly roared to life, indicating a full power go-around. Seconds later the twin was climbing away. The only traces of his passage were two small clouds of dust swirling just above the runway.

"Man, oh man!" "That was really close!" "I wouldn't have believed he'd get away with that!" The comments came thick and fast.

The twin went back around the landing pattern, lowered his gear, landed normally, and taxied up to the parking area by the terminal.

Several of us walked over to talk to the pilot about his narrow escape, and as he shut down the engines we saw that he *hadn't* escaped.

Several inches of each propeller blade were turned under. The prop tips striking the asphalt had caused the dust on the runway.

The pilot was on an Alaska Airlines 737 the next day, headed for Seattle. Gear-up landings are a no-no.

Oops!

Hoonah gets a lot of fog, so boaters and pilots have to learn to live with it. A good friend and fellow Sitka High School teacher, Al Decker, had lived and taught in Hoonah for some years before moving to Sitka. In those years Hoonah had no airport and was served by amphibious aircraft, PBYs and Grumman Gooses, just like most of the other towns in Southeast Alaska.

My friend Al spent his summers commercial fishing. He had a large 24 ft. wooden skiff with a 40 h.p. outboard engine, and occupied his days by jigging for halibut. He would tie two big halibut hooks on very heavy leaders, attach the leaders to the end of a light nylon rope just above a heavy sinker, bait each hook with a herring, and jig the baits up and down along the ocean bottom. He caught a lot of halibut that way, and made a fair summer wage.

One calm morning he was drifting and jigging north of Spaski Island when the fog rolled in. Shortly it was as thick as pea soup, and he had no idea which way home was, but he reasoned the fog would probably lift again before too long, so he just kept fishing.

After awhile he heard an airplane, and thought, "Surely no one is flying in this fog." Indeed, no one was flying. It soon became evident to Al that it was a Goose, and it was step-taxiing on the water. Apparently the pilot had landed somewhere out in Icy Straits and was high-speed-taxiing, headed for Hoonah in the fog.

The sound drew closer and closer, and Al began to get concerned. It sounded like it was coming in his direction.

The Goose broke out of the fog right on top of Al, and was headed directly at him. Al dived into the bottom of his skiff as the Grumman pilot goosed (*there's another one of those* terrible *puns!*) his engines, hopped neatly over Al's skiff, clearing it by mere inches, and then settled back down on the water.

When Al raised his head, the fog had swallowed the Goose again, and Al was laying face down in a pile of slimy halibut, plus several inches of water that the Goose had generously deposited in his skiff.

❧

Before the first flight of each morning an air taxi pilot preflights his airplane. We look at the tires, brakes, control surfaces, access plates, propeller, cowling fasteners, oil level, fuel level and drain the tank sumps to make sure no water condensed in the tanks over night. The object is to make sure the aircraft is safe for flight. Normally that's it for the day, except for adding fuel and oil, unless you change airplanes. Then you preflight the new one just like you did the previous one.

Boyd Hoops, our chief pilot, walked with me through my preflight inspection one morning, and when I finished he said "Are you usually that thorough with your preflights?"

"Well, yeah," I said. "I have to defy gravity with this thing, and I want to make sure it's capable." I thought that *he* thought I was being extra careful just because he was watching.

"Good. Now let me show you one more thing that you should probably check." He went over and put his shoulder under the propeller spinner and lifted up a little bit. The whole airplane rocked up with his effort.

I looked at him questioningly. He smiled and said "That's just to make sure the engine isn't going to fall out. See you in Juneau." and walked over to his airplane and got in.

Boyd has flown all his life, and has almost 20,000 hours in his logbooks, and as far as I know hasn't even kept a logbook for the last five years. He was born with wings, so if he wanted me to push up on the engine as part of my regular preflight inspection, I would jolly well push up on the engine, "just to make sure it wasn't going to fall out."

The following summer Cheryl assigned me a GBT in 808, the high wing Cessna 182. I had been flying 56 November, a Cherokee Six, so when we got to the airport I preflighted 808, and when I put my shoulder under her spinner and lifted, the engine raised six inches, but the airplane didn't raise at all ... it felt like I'd lifted the engine clear out of the airplane. What in the world ... ?

I unfastened the cowling and the problem was immediately obvious. Both front engine mounts were broken. A sudden application of full power could have easily developed enough torque that the engine would have twisted right out of the airplane.

Oops! (*Thanks, Boyd. I appreciate that ... a lot!*)

❧

Since we're on the subject of preflight inspections - it's amazing some of the things that can be overlooked on a preflight.

I was shooting touch-and-gos at the airport one spring day, and saw one of our competition's vans pull up next to a line of several of their company's planes. I won't tell you the name of the company, but I could give you their initials.

I recognized the company's check pilot, whom I was acquainted with, as he and a much younger man that I took to be a new pilot about to take a check ride, got out and walked over toward one of the airplanes.

I wasn't paying them a lot of attention as I continued with my touch-and-gos. I just wanted to know when they taxied for takeoff so I'd be aware of the increase in traffic.

I did three or four more circuits before I noticed that they had pulled out and started to taxi to the runway, and they were dragging one of those blue plastic tarps that are so common in Alaska. It must have been one of the bigger tarps, because it was wrapped around their nose wheel, and was trailing clear back behind the wings on both sides.

About then the chief pilot radioed, "Haines traffic, 21 Delta departing runway 8, staying in the pattern."

I responded "21 Delta, do NOT take off. You're dragging a tarp. DO NOT TAKE OFF!"

Two One Delta kept taxiing, and was already making the turn onto the active runway.

"TWO ONE DELTA! TWO ONE DELTA! DO NOT TAKE OFF! DO NOT TAKE OFF! YOU'RE DRAGGING A TARP WITH YOUR NOSE GEAR!"

I think it was the younger fellow who finally got the message. Two One Delta started to accelerate for a ways, and then throttled back and taxied to the next intersection and turned off the runway. The last I saw 21 Delta it was stopped in the middle of the taxiway, and both people were pulling on the tarp trying to get it loose from the nose wheel.

Oops! Must have missed that tarp during the preflight.

Cheryl Lowden, one of our dispatchers in Haines, has the most beautiful, smooth, melodious, soothing telephone voice I think I've ever heard. I just love to talk to her on the phone, so one day when I finished delivering some charter passengers to Gustavus, I went in and called the Haines office to find out what I was supposed to do next. Besides, it was a good excuse to hear Cheryl on the phone.

Her beautiful, smooth, melodious, soothing voice was pitched just a tad higher than normal. Apparently the dispatch situation was disintegrating around her, as it can often do in the air taxi business. She had airplanes scattered all over northern Southeast Alaska, but she needed them there in Haines ... and she needed them RIGHT NOW!

"Come as fast as you can, Cap'n Bob! I need you up here an hour ago!"

I ran out to the plane and took off from Gustavus, making a right turn to head up into Glacier Bay. The ceiling was somewhere around 3,000 feet, so I couldn't go directly over the top. The fastest route was to fly up Glacier Bay to the Endicott River, follow the Endicott Valley out to Lynn Canal, and then on to Haines.

I was making good time, but it's quite a distance from GST to HNS, and right after I passed the middle of the Endicott valley I spied a "shortcut."

The Endicott River flows between two steep mountain ridges averaging probably 3500 feet high, but at one spot the northern ridge has a fair-sized dip in it. On this day the ridge tops were solidly in cloud, but the dip came down to just below cloud level. There was a short gap of about 100 feet high and a quarter of a mile wide. I could see the Lynn Canal beaches through the gap.

"I don't have any passengers to worry about," I reasoned, "and if I shoot through this gap, I'll save 10 miles or more, and get to Haines that much faster."

I turned slightly left and aimed at the center of the gap. The gap across the ridge top looked perfectly clear. I'd cross the ridge with about 50 feet to spare.

Just as I roared up to the ridge I realized it *wasn't* perfectly clear. There was a little depression right along the top of the ridge, and there must have been twenty mountain goats resting in that shallow little bowl.

I was in a Cherokee Six, cruising at about 165 mph, so out of nowhere comes this howling, thundering monster, right over their heads. Those poor goats flushed like a covey of quail. A couple of them jumped so high it's a wonder I didn't hit them.

It was over in a flash, at least for me, but I wouldn't be surprised if some of those goats are *still* talking about it.

Oops! (*Sorry, goats. I really didn't do that to you on purpose.*)

It was a really pretty little helicopter. It was only a two-place ship, but it was great fun to fly. He'd gone Outside for training, but didn't have all that many helicopter hours yet, so he was really eager to fly it every chance he got.

He came out to the airport one day to get some more time in his little swing-wing. He jumped out of his truck, preflighted the 'copter, untied the pilot-side skid, and jumped in.

He carefully ran through the pre-takeoff checklist, started the engine, and lifted off to taxi to the runway.

Since the passenger-side skid was still tied down, the noise was tremendous when the little ship went over on her side and the rotor blades started taking big divots out of the pavement. There was lots of bent hardware, lots of assorted bits and pieces scattered about, and lots of bruised ego, but thankfully no physical injuries to the pilot.

Oops!

Every commercial airplane, whether it carries one person or four hundred, has to have a mandatory inspection every 100 flight hours. This is normally referred to as a "hundred hour."

By this time Haines Airways had eight airplanes, its own maintenance hangar, and its own mechanics. The airplanes ranged from 70 Lima and 808, both four-place aircraft, up to 726, a ten-place IFR-equipped twin-engine Piper Chieftain, irreverently nicknamed "The Pig."

The Pig was parked out on the ramp, having just come out of the hangar after a hundred hour. Jim, one of the mechanics, was performing the last few items on the hundred hour check list. One of the items involved running the engines up to approximately 2,000 rpm and checking mags, manifold pressure and several other things.

Jim had the parking brakes set, and The Pig was sitting there throbbing and vibrating with both engines at half-throttle while Jim ran through his check list.

One other item that needed to be checked, although not expressly at this particular time, was the operation of the landing gear's dead switch. Moving a small lever on the center console from "down" to "up" normally retracts the aircraft's landing gear. The dead switch keeps this lever from functioning when the aircraft is sitting on the ground; in other words, it prevents the pilot from accidentally retracting the landing gear until the plane is actually airborne.

Jim was kneeling on the floor, and right in front of his nose was the landing gear lever, and the dead switch access panel. "Might as well check out the dead switch while I'm here," thinks Jim, so he opens the dead switch access panel, pulls the landing gear lever back, and finds out ... the dead switch appears to be defective.

He's pretty sure the dead switch isn't working properly because The Pig has just retracted its gear, settled 3 feet onto its belly, and $135,000 worth of aircraft engines and props are busy chewing large bites of asphalt out of the parking area surface and thrashing themselves into total ruin.

Oops! And double oops! Don't you just *hate* it when that happens?

"Juneau Tower, Admiralty Air 25 Delta approaching Outer Point for a landing in Juneau. Request Special VFR clearance."

Steve had been flying in Southeast Alaska for a number of years, and was well-known and well-thought-of by tower controllers as well as by many air taxi personnel, both pilots and ground employees.

It had been marginal flying weather for most of the day. The cool air temperature and the warm moist ocean air combined to form lots of low thick fog. The wind was calm, so there was nothing to dispel the fog. One or two Alaska Airlines jets had made it into Juneau earlier, but others had overflown or diverted to other destinations. Several air taxi flights had come in or departed under Special VFR clearances, so Steve's request for a "special" wasn't particularly noteworthy.

However, as the controller prepared to give Steve his requested special clearance, he was electrified to hear Steve's tardy addendum. "Oh, by the way, could you have the crash truck stand by? I've had a little accident."

That got the immediate attention of everyone in the tower. As people grabbed binoculars and started scanning the fog-filled sky for 25 Delta, the crash truck rolled out of the airport fire hall, lights flashing and siren wailing, and headed for the approach end of the runway.

Soon one of the controllers spotted 25 Delta staggering through the fog towards the runway. It was immediately obvious that something really serious had occurred. The low-winged Cherokee was on final approach, flying slowly and erratically, with one wing drooping significantly and the other raised. From a mile away the controllers could see a huge lump on 25 Delta's lowered wing.

Steve managed to land the airplane without digging the lowered wing into the runway, so once his roll-out was completed and there was no sign of fire, the immediate emergency was over. The crash truck rolled along beside Steve, while the ground controller cleared 25 Delta to "taxi to parking."

"Nah." responded Steve. "I'd like to taxi to Southeast Aviation's shop. I think they're going to need to look at this." The crash truck escorted Steve to the shop and then continued on back to the fire hall.

Steve had barely shut the engine off before a small crowd of mechanics and office workers from Southeast Aviation gathered around to examine the damaged Cherokee and hear Steve's story.

The damaged wing had obviously collided with something. The leading edge was pushed all the way back to the main spar, creating a huge bulge in the wing. The damaged area, roughly diamond-shaped, was over four feet wide and two feet thick. In addition to destroying any lift in that part of the wing, the bulge created a huge amount of drag. No wonder 25 Delta was flying with one wing low. It was a wonder that it was still flying at all.

Steve was a quiet, slow-speaking fellow, so it took awhile for his audience to draw out the story.

It seems that Steve got caught in dense fog on his way from Hoonah to Juneau. As he crossed Chatham Straits the fog forced him lower and lower.

As he entered Funter Bay he decided to turn around, but the fog had closed in behind him, so he had no choice but to turn again and keep heading for Juneau. By the time he reached the head of Funter Bay he was right down at tree-top level, and knew that his only choice was to try to follow Bear Creek drainage across the Mansfield Peninsula to Stephens Passage and then hopefully on across Stephens Passage to Auke Bay and Juneau.

Near the summit of Bear Creek Pass the fog was so thick that all he could see was the tops of spruce trees flashing by just below his wing.

"All of a sudden an eagle came out of nowhere," Steve said, and slammed right into my wing. It just about scared me to death. I just barely managed to keep control. I had to keep it at nearly full throttle just to stay in the air."

Steve had just finished his story when the FAA reps showed

up. Tower personnel had notified them of the accident, so several of them came over to investigate.

Steve had to repeat his story for the FAA and answer many questions so they could get all the required information for their report. When they heard that he had hit an eagle, they decided that the local Federal Fish and Wildlife agent should be notified. A quick phone call confirmed that another report would be necessary, as the bald eagle is on the endangered species list.

The fog had lifted quite a bit by then. I had just landed in Juneau, heard about all the excitement, and walked over to view the damage for myself. I arrived shortly after the Federal Fish and Wildlife agent, so I heard most of Steve's third account of the accident.

The Fish and Wildlife man eventually got all the information he needed (*or perhaps just satisfied his own curiosity*) and left.

There were just a couple of latecomers like myself remaining. Steve ambled over to us as we continued to survey the damage.

A couple of commiserating comments were made - "Boy, you sure were lucky!" and "Man, what a story!" kinds of remarks.

Steve gazed thoughtfully at the mutilated wing on his airplane, and then in his quiet, slow talking way responded "Well, fellas, I just don't know. Do you think I should have mentioned to those federal guys that the eagle was sitting in a tree when I hit him?"

Oops!

# Chapter Twenty Seven
## DITCHING AT SKAGWAY

Susan was returning her five elderly passengers to their tour ship in Skagway. It was a beautiful August afternoon, and she was bringing her passengers back from a very successful Nature Tour flight. Six or seven other airplanes were also involved. Some were ahead of her, and some followed.

She was two or three miles out of Skagway, descending to pattern altitude, when her engine quit ... just stopped dead, without a cough or whimper.

She tried restarting procedures, but the engine wouldn't even turn over again. At the same time she was broadcasting on the Skagway CTAF - "Mayday, Mayday, Mayday. My engine's quit and I'm going down."

Other aircraft scurried to get out of her way, so she was clear no matter what course of action she chose to take. A nearby local sightseeing helicopter followed her down. She saw that she could not possibly glide to the runway, in fact she couldn't glide to any land. She was going to have to ditch in the water.

She briefed her passengers to get life jackets out of the seat pockets in front of them, and made sure both front and back cabin doors were unlatched and ready to open. By the time she'd done that she was immediately faced with ditching the aircraft.

The water landing was entirely successful. All six passengers got out of the aircraft under their own power, and the helicopter was almost immediately overhead, sprinkling life vests liberally over the swimmers.

In spite of this, two passengers sank and were lost in the cold waters of Taiya Inlet, and another two were dead when a rescue craft arrived a few minutes later. Susan and another woman survived.

The aircraft was raised from 75 feet of water two weeks later. The NTSB investigation concluded that a magneto had been faultily repaired at the factory. The mag came apart in flight, shed parts and pieces into the engine's camshaft assembly, and ultimately caused the engine to fail catastrophically.

Susan's water landing was so gentle that the majority of the damage to the aircraft was caused by the cables and winches used to raise the plane from the ocean bottom.

The NTSB Accident Investigation Report (8) states:

The National Transportation Safety Board determines the probable cause(s) of this accident as follows:

JAMMING/FAILURE OF THE LEFT MAGNETO IM-PULSE COUPLING, WHICH STOPPED ROTATION OF THE MAGNETO GEAR, AND RESULTED IN SUBSE-QUENT SHEARING OF THE ACCESSORY INTERMEDI-ATE IDLER GEAR. FACTORS RELATING TO THE ACCI-DENT WERE: THE LACK OF SUITABLE TERRAIN FOR A FORCED LANDING, WHICH NECESSITATED DITCH-ING OF THE AIRCRAFT; THE PASSENGER'S LACK OF AWARENESS CONCERNING ACCESS TO LIFE VESTS, DUE TO THE PILOT'S INADEQUATE BRIEFING AND THE SEAT COVERS BEING INSTALLED OVER POUCH-ES THAT HELD THE LIFE VESTS; INSUFFICIENT COMPANY STANDARDS/PROCEDURES REGARDING ACCESS TO LIFE VESTS.

# Chapter Twenty Eight
## HOT DOGƒ AND REAL FIGHTER PILOTƒ

By the time we finished with our FlyCruise duties and got everything squared away for the flight home to Haines it was getting pretty dark. It was mid-August, there was a high overcast, and a brisk north wind blowing down the Canal toward us. It had been a pretty big FlyCruise, so there were a number of planes deadheading back up north for either Haines or Skagway. We would all be arriving home just about the time it got totally dark.

I tuned to Juneau Ground just in time to hear another company's young pilot request "Taxi to active with flight of three." Permission was granted, and I saw three of our competitor's Cherokees taxi out together.

I was cleared to taxi right behind them, and as we neared the active runway I heard them tell the tower that they were "ready for takeoff, flight of three," and so they departed, one right after the other, as a flight.

I took off next, and by the time I had I cleared the control zone and rounded Lena Point I had climbed to 1,500 feet and was cruising for home.

I hadn't seen the flight of three since they lifted off, and started to search, wondering where they were. I knew they were three young, relatively inexperienced pilots, so I wouldn't put anything past them.

I finally found them in the murky twilight; three sets of lights, very close together, and very low on the water. They were almost under my nose, at least 1,000 feet below me.

As I watched, the set of lights on the left slowly turned from red to green to red! Then the set of lights on the right turned from red to green to red, and then the middle set did the same thing. Those three clowns were down at low level, over water, on a windy night, in almost pitch dark, doing barrel rolls in Cherokee Sixes, in formation.

They hadn't been talking on the Lynn Canal CTAF, so I figured they must be on their company's discrete pilot frequency, an "informal" frequency the pilots from that particular company used, usually when the pilots were involved in something they didn't want to broadcast to either their boss or the world in general. Every air taxi company has its own discrete frequency.

I switched to that frequency, and sure enough, there they were, giggling and carrying on like they had good sense.

Their company's chief pilot has a really gruff radio voice, so I keyed my transmitter and growled, loud and rapid-fire, "You so-and-so's get those airplanes apart and up where they belong NOW! If I catch you doing rolls in a company airplane again I'll ship you so far away your own mother will never find you!"

The effect was instantaneous! Poof! They split apart and popped up like ducks flushed from a farm pond.

They didn't utter another word all the way home ... and neither did I.

As the SkagAir sightseeing plane came out of the Katzaheen Glacier valley, the pilot heard "There's one of them. Let's get him!" on the CTAF.

Searching around, he spotted two airplanes from a rival company in loose formation just ahead and above him. One of them peeled off in a shallow dive and came streaking towards him. Apparently this was supposed to be some kind of overhead gunnery pass. The SkagAir pilot was not amused, and said, "Hey you guys, I've got passengers. This isn't funny. Knock it off."

The CTAF reverberated with vibrating lips - "Rata-tat-tat-tat" - as the first plane passed a couple of hundred feet overhead.

The second plane was close behind the first, and the "firing pass" was repeated.

The SkagAir pilot was not amused. His passengers were even less amused.

The FAA Safety Inspector who happened to be riding in the right front seat with SkagAir, the one with the two aircraft N numbers now written in his notebook, was downright hostile, and his mood hadn't improved much when he confronted the two "aces" later that afternoon.

The two hotdogs caught the red-eye flight from Juneau to Seattle that night, their ears still burning, and their pilot's licenses tucked securely in the FAA inspector's pocket.

The air taxi business doesn't need fighter jocks, it needs careful, competent pilots.

I met a lot of other aviators when I was flying air taxi. I met pilots who flew for our company, for SkagAir *(our "sister" company)*, or for our competition. But there were also lots of other pilots and ex-pilots who had flown bush, commuter, airline and/or military planes. Without fail they were interesting to meet and swap tales with. Here are a couple of the more memorable military stories.

The two young foreign women, in their mid- to late 20s, booked themselves onto a GBT that had already been scheduled by a couple of semi-professional photographers, so when we got to the airport and seat assignments were made, the photographers had first choice, and they chose the back row, as it has the most unobstructed view from a Cherokee Six.

The author at the controls of 36 Romeo, on a Glacier Bay tour. August, 1992
(note: this photo was digitally repaired, due to water damage)

One young lady, fairly attractive and speaking fluent English, sat in the middle row by herself, and indicated to her companion that she should sit up front with me.

The companion apparently spoke only a little English, but she was a beauty with a capital "B." With short black hair, olive complexion, and stunningly attractive, she could have been in the Sports

Illustrated Swim Suit Edition with no problem.

We went to Glacier Bay and spent our hour enthusiastically looking for wildlife and cruising the glaciers, and then returned to Haines. On the way back to town in the van I asked the English-speaker where they were from.

"Israel," she replied.

Her friend said something to her, and she looked at me and translated, "My friend wants me to tell you that she *really* enjoyed the flight.

"Good, I always like to hear that folks felt the trip was worth-while."

"My friend flies too, you know." she remarked.

"Oh really," I replied. I wasn't aware that Israel had much of a civil aviation program. It's such a small country. I turned to the pretty one and asked, "What kind of airplane do you usually fly?"

She actually blushed, shyly glanced down for a second, and then looked back at me and very charmingly said ... "F-15s."

Oh!

*I related this story to another Israeli a few of years later, a middle aged macho-sort, and he scoffed and said, "She was pulling your leg." I'll leave it for you to decide, but that's exactly what she said.*

We had just landed in Skagway after finishing a Nature Tour flight. I was walking my five passengers to their bus when one of the older gentlemen, short and stocky, but trim and fit, came up beside me and said in a pronounced German accent, "Dot vas a wery enchoyable flight." He hesitated a moment and then continued "I uzed to fly also."

I suspected what his answer was going to be, but I asked anyway. "What did you fly?"

He straightened up just a bit, lifted his chin, and said "Messer-schmitts. ME 109s. "

I was just about to respond with some inane comment like "Oh, that's interesting," when a distinctly British accent right behind me asked, "I say then, I wonder if we've ever met before?"

The Brit, tall and lean, with a snow-white mustache and wavy white hair, stepped forward and looked down at the German. "I flew Spitfires, you know."

The German looked at the Brit for several seconds, and then without a word turned on his heel and climbed into the bus.

The Brit watched him board the bus, then turned to me, and said, "Seems like perhaps we *have* met before, what?" ... and winked.

He was a tall man, probably 6'3" or 6'4." From his thinning gray hair and weathered face I estimated him to be in his mid-seventies. He didn't speak a word of English, apparently. There were five of them altogether, two older couples and one younger man who spoke fluent English. The younger man appeared to be the official guide.

They were part of a larger party, about 20 people altogether, all from Germany. They were "experiencing" Alaska, and had chartered with Haines Airways to take the entire party from Juneau to Gustavus, so we had four airplanes and pilots involved. Their guide said the group would spend three days doing different trips up into Glacier Bay, and then would catch the Alaska Airlines jet that went on to Anchorage.

I escorted my five passengers out to the airplane, and as I started seating folks this tall fellow was having a discussion with the guide. The guide then turned to me and said, "He wants to sit up front with you."

"No problem," I replied. "He just has to get in last, after me."

The guide and I got everyone seated and belted in, ran through a bi-lingual passenger briefing, taxied, and departed Juneau.

It was a beautiful day, so I commented on some of the scenic points of interest, and the guide translated for the others. I noticed, though, that the man in front with me was paying little attention to our surroundings. He was watching me, and the instrument panel, like a hawk.

"Mmm hmm," I thought. "I'll bet this man has a story to tell."

After we landed in Gustavus I taxied to the parking area, unloaded passengers and baggage, and then led the folks over to their bus.

Most of the party was aboard the bus when the tall man turned around and came back to where I was standing.

"Ich fliege auch," he said softly. (*I flew also.*)

My single year of high school German, much mellowed by 35 years of passing time, kicked in and I replied "Ah. Was fliegen Zie?" (*Oh. What did you fly?*)

"Stuka," came the reply. (*WW II German dive bomber.*)

"Ach, du fliegen der Stuka? Fliegen sie mit Rudel?" (*Oh, you flew a Stuka? Did you fly with Rudel?*)

*I had very recently finished reading* "Stuka Pilot," *the autobiography of Hans Ulrich Rudel, a very famous German dive bomber pilot and Germany's most decorated World War II hero, so his name came immediately to mind.*

His eyes got wide, and I could see tears well up in them. He grabbed my right hand in both of his, and shook it, obviously very emotional.

"Yah, yah! Er hat mein Kommandeur. Er hat mein Kommandeur." *(Yes, yes! He was my commanding officer.)*

Tears were running down both cheeks as he continued to shake my hand.

A woman stuck her head out the bus door and called "Fritz, kommen sie, bitte. Schnell." *(Fritz, come on, please. Hurry.)*

He stopped at the bus door and called back to me "Danke. Viele Danke. Auf Wiedersehen." *(Thanks. Many thanks. Goodbye.)*

# Chapter Twenty Nine
## LAST FLIGHT

On July 31, 1997, I flew 4.7 hours in Cherokee Six PA-32-300, N8991 November. I landed in Haines, Juneau, Hoonah, Skagway, and Gustavus. I carried a total of 23 passengers. The weather was calm with a high broken overcast.

It was supposed to be my last day of flying for a while. I had some medical issues that required further tests in Seattle, so I had arranged for a couple of weeks off.

That evening, after making my daily logbook entry, I turned the page and realized that my third logbook was full. I mentioned it to my wife, and she responded with "That's enough. The season will be nearly over by the time we get back from Seattle, and I really would rather that you didn't fly again next summer. Tell them you've used up all your safe landings."

I had retired from education a year earlier, and Aleta wanted me to retire completely, so we would be free to travel, visit family in the Lower 48, and spend time pursuing some of our other interests.

I wasn't overly pleased with the direction the company had been taking lately anyway, so after thinking it over I agreed with her, and notified the office that my "short leave" would be permanent.

That summer Haines Airways was experiencing a new owner, an "absentee landlord," who had over-hired personnel, over-purchased equipment, and was soon over-his-head in financial difficulties. The company was sold again shortly after I retired and the next buyer, a large air taxi company in Juneau, liquidated all of Haines Airways' equipment and put the company's air taxi certificate up on a shelf. That's one way to eliminate competition.

Personally, I logged well over 3,500 hours, most of it air taxi time in Southeast. I met and worked with some wonderful people, and had one of the most enjoyable and rewarding summer jobs a person could possibly have, flying over some of the most incredibly beautiful country in the world.

Some of my fellow Haines Airways pilots went on to the "majors," and are now airline captains and first officers flying "heavy iron" around the nation and around the world. One is chief pilot for a large air taxi company in Juneau. One flies a jet air ambulance. Another has his own air taxi business. Others are corporate pilots for large companies in the Lower 48. Some have dropped out of aviation and are managing profitable businesses or having successful careers in other fields. One or two are no longer in aviation and are bagging groceries or pumping gas, where they belong. Others are no longer living, some dying in airplanes and others dying in bed.

My friend Ernie Walker is currently a Safety Inspector for the FAA, based in Anchorage.

I'm glad I got to fly with all of them. Every single one of them taught me something about flying, and something about life.

I'm extremely pleased that I was able to realize my boyhood dream of taking wing. Many, many thanks to all the folks who made that dream a reality, and who made my flying career so memorable.

I often sit and recall those days. Many of those experiences are indelibly inscribed in my memory; some because of the sheer beauty of the country and the exhilaration of the freedom of flight, and others because of the hair-raising nature of the conditions that had to be faced. Some were memorable simply because of the foibles of human nature that were involved. Some were hilariously amusing, and others were tremendously sobering. I value each and every one.

During my flying years I got to fly about two dozen different types of aircraft. I flew tiny 90 hp Champs and doggish Cessna 150s. I flew a stock Cessna 170B with its soft, springy landing gear. I flew a 170B with a 180 hp Lycoming (*99 Charlie on mega-vitamins*), and I flew a 170B with a 210 hp engine and constant speed prop (*99 Charlie on steroids*), but I never flew in one I liked better than 99 Charlie. I flew Stinsons, Aeroncas, Cessna 140s, 180s, 182s, and 206s. I logged many hours in Cherokee Sixes, an airplane that I detested when I first flew it, but experience caused me to develop a real affection and appreciation for it. I also liked flying the Piper Seminole, a twin-engine version of the Cherokee Six. The largest aircraft I ever flew was "The Pig," Haines Airways' ten-place twin engine Piper Chieftain.

Poor 99 Charlie ended up upside down on top of Tsirku Glacier. The pilot, flying under a low overcast, misjudged his distance above the surface of the glacier, and flew right into the soft snow. The pilot wasn't hurt (*except for his ego and his wallet*), but Charlie took a real beating.

Occasionally now, on a beautiful summer day, I'll think to myself "I'd sure like to go flying today," but those kinds of summer days are rare in Southeast Alaska. Sometimes when I'm up early in the morning I'll look out at the mountains and see those beautiful streaky layers of cloud and fog that are so typical of Southeast, and remember what it was like on those early morning trips up and down Lynn Canal, but more often I think, as I see some hapless air taxi driver bouncing and skidding sideways through the wind and rain and mist, "I'm sure glad it's him up there today, and not me."

Haines Airways is gone from the air taxi scene. The maintenance hangar at the airport still has the Haines Airways logo painted on the side, but the building hasn't been used in several years. The office in downtown Haines now houses a museum. Another air taxi business occupies our old space in the Juneau airport.

Skagway Air Service closed its doors in the summer of 2007, after 43 years of service. Mike O'Daniel reached retirement age and simply pulled the plug, shutting down flight operations, selling off the company assets, and calling it quits.

The FAA revoked another local company's air taxi certificate in July 2008 for "continued improper maintenance and compliance problems." The company, which first started commercial operations in 1956, had been under Federal scrutiny for over six years, and had already paid approximately $60,000 in fines for repeatedly violating FAA safety regulations. Authorities at the FAA said that "based on the evidence gathered in their report, it's unlikely that XXX will be back in the air ..."

Several other regional flying services have expressed interest in expanding to fill the gap left by these closures.

Most of the people that I worked with, pilots and ground personnel, aren't here any more. Many have simply moved away, but some are gone forever. Occasionally I see one of the old gang, but rarely do we talk about "the good old days." For many of us those flying days are over, but they're not forgotten, and in Southeast Alaska, the wild and magnificent land that is still so dependent on air travel, there will always be a new crop of young and not so young pilots seeking to try their wings.

Good luck and best wishes to them all. Fly safe.

As the Stuka pilot said, "Auf Wiedersehen."

HainesAir 56 November on a Glacier Bay tour.
Glacier Bay National Park – Summer, 1995

# BIBLIOGRAPHY

1) National Transportation Safety Board -
   Aviation Accident Database Query - Index of Months
   *http://www.ntsb,gov/ntsb/month.asp*,  October 16, 1972

2) NTSB - Aviation Accident Database,  February 15, 1984

3) NTSB - Aviation Accident Database,  September 20, 1981

4) NTSB - Aviation Accident Database,  July 30, 1989

5) NTSB - Aviation Accident Database,  May 18, 1976

6) NTSB - Aviation Accident Database,  July 7, 1995

7) NTSB - Aviation Accident Database,  August 14, 1991

8) NTSB - Aviation Accident Database,  July 3, 1997

# ABOUT THE AUTHOR

BOB ADKINS moved to Alaska from Michigan in 1964 and spent 32 years in public education in Sitka, Anchorage, and Haines. He has degrees in engineering, math and physics, counseling and school administration. He also spent 14 seasons as captain of his own commercial fishing boat in Bristol Bay and Lynn Canal, and 12 summers as an air taxi pilot in Southeast Alaska. He holds a commercial pilot's license and has single engine sea, single engine land, multi-engine land and instrument ratings. During his active flying years he was a certified flight instructor.

Bob is also a self-taught photographer, and since retiring from education in 1996 has photographed in Alaska, the Yukon, the Pacific Northwest, England, Europe and southern Africa. His numerous articles and photos have appeared in over twenty different publications, including *WildBird, Outdoor Photographer, Emergency, Alaska Magazine, AAA Home & Away, Birder's World, TWA Ambassador, The Milepost, Fur, Fish, & Game, Nature Photographer, Sports Afield, African Hunting Gazette* and *Parade Magazine*. His photos have also appeared in news journals from coast to coast and in Europe, as well as in books and on international calendars and CD covers. He recently served as a contract still photographer for The History Channel, and is currently a field contributor to Nature Photographer magazine.

His previous book, *THE GOLDEN CIRCLE: Over 100 Photographs From Gold Rush Country* (ISBN 1-59152-020-7) was published in 2005, and is available at gift shops and book stores throughout Alaska and the Yukon Territory, and also through the author's website:

http://www.bobadkinsphotography.com

Bob and his wife Aleta have lived in Haines, Alaska since 1974.